Each recovered text has its own texture and size. We'll never know what the complete books looked like—these pages are all that remain.

—LUKE

# BOOK OF

## Sith

## SECRETS FROM THE DARK SIDE

# PREFACE

By Darth Sidious

I have accomplished what no Sith has ever done before. I have destroyed the Jedi and subverted Coruscant. I sit on the throne of a new and unstoppable regime. I will shape the great Galactic Empire according to my own design.

The Sith have dreamt of this moment since the beginning of recorded history. I could not have achieved this prize without treading on the backs of those who came before. Exploiting the failures of others is the way of the Sith.

Since my days as a young noble on Naboo, long before I joined Darth Plagueis and began my apprenticeship, I collected dark side lore. These rubbings of Sith tablets and untranslatable runic scrolls were coveted and traded on the black markets by cultists, collectors, and museum curators willing to defy the Republic's ban on Sith artifacts.

The very existence of this illicit trade confirms many vital truths: Rulers seek to control information. The powerful will do anything to hoard their power. And if something is forbidden, it is likely a thing worth knowing.

Getting these artifacts past the law officials and into my quarters on Naboo provided new lessons: True power brokers dwell in the shadows. Credits can buy anything, even intangible concepts such as access and silence. It is necessary to lie to achieve anything of value. And a skilled liar is nearly impossible to detect.

Although my experience acquiring the texts provided a practical knowledge of how treasures and secrets change hands, as well as the roles non-Force sensitives play in keeping the galaxy running, the actual dark side tomes deepened my knowledge of the ancient Sith. I realized that I had all the tools I needed to craft my own system of power, one that fused contemporary politics with Sith ideals.

Under the tutelage of Darth Plagueis, I inherited the Sith Archives—more than a thousand years' worth of teachings passed in secret from master to apprentice. But what I learned was that only a handful of figures had ever truly advanced the cause of the Sith. Thus I made it my goal to recover their most famous writings—not the revisions of misguided chroniclers who lived hundreds of years after them but the parchments bearing their original words and recorded by their own hands. With the fall of the Jedi Temple, I have finally recovered the last of these documents, though only fragments of each have survived the centuries.

Together these pages unite one of the first Sith Lords with he who shall be the last. Each author's voice echoes the era in which he or she held power, but the Sith Order has evolved over seven thousand years. The errors made by my predecessors will not be my own. Their triumphs will be nothing compared to my omnipotence.

*At the time I wrote these words, I hoped my Empire would provide limitless reach. Yet I must still rely on others to do my bidding. And they are so often foolish, flawed, and disappointing.*

# THE NEW TRUTHS

Every holocron I've studied and every new dark side cult simply restates the teachings of the Sith encapsulated in these texts. But Sorzus Syn, Darth Malgus, Darth Bane, Mother Talzin, and Darth Plagueis believed too rigidly in their own dogmas. If any of them could have met and shared their beliefs, they would have found little common ground.

I have bound the recovered pages from the works of these great Sith Lords in one volume. These relics are unique and irreplaceable—they are the *Book of Sith*.

Sorzus Syn's chronicle of the rise of the Sith Empire is the oldest text by many thousands of years. She was a Dark Jedi banished into exile following their failed war against the Jedi. Syn was exceptionally adept at twisting life through Sith alchemy. The Jedi kept these pages locked in their Archives, but I reclaimed them after the cleansing of their Temple. Regrettably, I could not remove the scrawls left in the margins by Jedi Masters Yoda and Mace Windu while the text was in their possession.

The excerpts from the journal of Darth Malgus kept during the Great Galactic War some thirty-six

The Dark Jedi exiles reached Sith Space circa 7,000 B.B.Y.; following the Hundred-Year Darkness. Sorzus Syn's writings appear to have been recorded at several points over the subsequent years. The comments of Yoda and Mace Windu are difficult to pin down, but most likely date from before the Battle of Naboo in 32 B.B.Y. —LUKE

centuries ago are a prime example of how a wounded warrior can be sustained by rage. The war was an unbounded success for the era's Sith Emperor, and Malgus was one of his best soldiers. I obtained this text many decades ago from a dealer in antiquities, and have recently passed it to Darth Vader so he might gain inspiration.

BANE SURVIVED THE BATTLE OF RUUSAN IN 1,000 B.B.Y. THIS TEXT MAY HAVE BEEN RECORDED A DECADE LATER, BUT THAT'S CONJECTURE. IT'S NOT KNOWN HOW LONG DARTH BANE LIVED. —LUKE

Darth Bane's *Rule of Two* was a keystone of the Sith Order for centuries. The Battle of Ruusan, nearly a millennium ago, would have ended the Sith Order had Darth Bane not reconstituted it as a diarchy operating from the shadows. His writings became part of the Sith Archives passed down from master to apprentice for generations. During the Clone Wars, my servant Count Dooku shared the book with Jedi agent Quinlan Vos in an ill-conceived effort to lure and corrupt him. Count Dooku's failure is no longer important, for my clone troopers rectified that breach and eliminated Vos while carrying out Order 66.

HAPPILY, THE EMPEROR SEEMS TO HAVE GOTTEN THIS ONE WRONG. I'VE READ ACCOUNTS THAT QUINLAN VOS SURVIVED AND WENT INTO HIDING DURING THE DARK TIMES. —LUKE

Most texts I recovered were penned by Sith, but *Wild Power* by Mother Talzin relates to another dark side group—the Nightsisters. Although Talzin's text expounds on her misguided reverence for nature spirits, it does possess a shrewd pragmatism I admire.

THE CHRONOLOGY OF THE CLONE WARS IS CONFUSING. I CAN'T BE MORE PRECISE THAN TO STATE THAT TALZIN'S WRITINGS AND VENTRESS'S COMMENTS DATE FROM THE TIME FRAME OF THAT CONFLICT. —LUKE

The members of her Nightsister clan became merchants for the galaxy's finest dark side mercenaries during the Clone Wars. Asajj Ventress, a Nightsister by birth who served Count Dooku until I ordered otherwise, appears to have added her commentary after she slinked away to Dathomir to become a member of the tribe once more. One of my Inquisitors recovered this book while raiding the planet to capture Force-sensitive slaves.

My Master, Darth Plagueis, recorded his own musings on what he believed to be the true nature of the dark side. Although he had a fatal blind spot, he revolutionized Sith understanding of the relationship between biology and the Force. The pages of this text still bear the comments I made after taking Darth Plagueis's place as Master and making his possessions my own.

The stories of the previous authors ended, but my reign is just beginning. By melding the core truths of the dark side found in these texts, I have set forth: The Book of Anger, The Weakness of Inferiors, and The Manipulation of Life.

These establish the true knowledge of the dark side and make plain the tasks required to implement a Sith Order.

*As my skill has deepened, I realize the applications of the Force are infinite. In time, these three books will become the cornerstone of my multi-volume Dark Side Compendium.*

*DARTH PLAGUEIS's TEXT MAY DATE FROM ROUGHLY 45 B.B.Y, BUT THAT'S ONLY AN EDUCATED GUESS. HIS DEATH MAY NOT HAVE OCCURRED UNTIL THE BATTLE OF NABOO IN 32 B.B.Y. AND IT IS STILL SOMETHING OF A MYSTERY HOW PALPATINE CAME TO STUDY THE WAYS OF THE SITH UNDER HIM. —LUKE*

*PALPATINE DID COMPLETE THESE VOLUMES, OR AT LEAST MADE A LOT OF PROGRESS. DURING MY TIME ON BYSS, I SAW HIS MANIFESTO IN THE RECORDS LIBRARY. BUT ONLY PARTIAL COPIES SEEM TO HAVE SURVIVED BYSS's DESTRUCTION. —LUKE*

# Exile and Arrival

I am not Sith. I do not share their blood. Yet, in the time since we arrived among these savage people, we have become their rulers. For the Force-strong must ever seek power. We have adopted their titles, their dress, and their traditions. We are no longer Jedi expelled from the Republic's smothering embrace. We are the Jen'jidai, Lords of the Sith.

We arrived here after the hundred-year war that nearly toppled their Jedi Order. The Jedi, so confident in their triumph, did not execute us. With lightsaber points at our backs, they marched us aboard the galleon that would take us into exile, outside the Republic's borders.

There were twelve of us, including several ranking commanders: High General Ajunta Pall; Marchioness XoXaan, commander of the Black Legions; Baron Dreypa, our fleet's sole remaining admiral; Karness Muur, whose Force-centered battle tactics had saved us from the trap at Fluwhaka; and I, Sorzus Syn, grower of living weapons and biological plagues. Other less distinguished Dark Jedi were prominent within our company only because they had not perished in the war.

The war had raged for a century between the Jedi Council, with its petrified orthodoxy, and those who wished to topple it. As the last survivors of those who sought a new path to power, we ultimately fell victim to the military excess of the Jedi at the Rout of Corbos.

Our punishment for high treason was to be banished into uncharted space. But our flight into the unknown was not without direction. For years, I extracted information from refugees and cataloged rumors, searching for proof that the kingdom of Sith—Sith Purebloods—existed. My beliefs have been vindicated. What lies before us is a limitless pool of steadfast warriors and an untapped wealth of knowledge about the dark side of the Force.

*XoXaan, myself, Ajunta Pall, and Dreypa—not our landing but rather our triumph over the Sith Purebloods marked our arrival.*

# The First Great Schism

We rule the Sith. Here we will build a sovereignty of the dark side to overcome millennia of injustice. But I am the rightful ruler, for I alone possess the curiosity to translate their secrets and apply them to larger patterns of conquest. I foresee what will become a magnificent Sith Empire.

While Corbos was the last battle of the Hundred-Year Darkness, the conflict began with the most recent Great Schism. Historians squabble over how many such splits have occurred within Jedi ranks. I care not for the exact number, but with each one, the Jedi Council's stranglehold on the ways of the Force weakened.

The Hundred-Year Darkness was a spectacular, yet predictable, revolt against Jedi complacency. The Jedi Order has not evolved in nearly twenty millennia. Even after the Order's founding on Tython, its most curious members realized the failings of their teachers—and so began the First Great Schism.

*Charge of the Black Legions at the Battle of Corbos*

*Not all who split with the Order became combatants; Jedi Masters who resigned the Order for philosophical reasons were perversely venerated, with bronzium busts in the Temple Archives commemorating them as "the Lost."*

*The dark side is not more powerful.*
*It burns bright, but quickly burns out.*
*Mace*

In those days, a Kashi Mer outsider named Xendor inspired several Jedi to question the light side, or Ashla. They discovered the use of the dark side, or Bogan, unlocked the shackles their Jedi Masters had placed on the Force. Xendor's followers—those who believed as he did but lacked his abilities—became his acolytes, or the Legions of Lettow.

Of course, the Jedi fought. They fought with desperation, against a future in which they had no followers. History says that Xendor and his legions perished in the Battle of Columus.

But that was not the tragedy of the First Great Schism. The tragedy was that the Jedi learned nothing. They could have embraced the dark side and become the central power of the Empire that the Legions of Lettow sought to build. Instead, they returned to their antiquated ways and alienated their most gifted members. We exiles are the heirs to Xendor's bold heresy.

*Compromise with the dark side? Defeat it is. Vigilant the Jedi must remain.*
*—Yoda*

Xendor and the Legions of Lettow defy the Jedi at Columus.

# The Hundred-Year Darkness

The war in which we fought, and in which many of our followers died, could have been prevented. It was the Jedi who took up arms to keep us from revealing the truth about the Force. They had been paddling in the shallows for eons. By boldly venturing into the Force's expanse, we gained powers that no Jedi had ever possessed. Life itself was at our command.

It was I who grew the Leviathans, who splintered the Jedi barricades at Balmorra. I gave them the ability to swallow spirits and to store those life energies in skin-blisters. The Leviathans, my exquisite monsters, were the final culmination of the Shamblers, the Howlers, the Pit Horrors, and all the other spawn I'd given shape and purpose to—my purpose.

The Jedi shunned this power, as they have resisted every improvement. They caused the schism in their own ranks. Until we annihilate the old Order, the pattern will continue repeating forever.

The Sith perversion of living things violates the very essence of the Force. Life creates it, allows us to tap its potential. We obey its will—not the other way around. We are parts of the organism, not its breeders. In the end we are living beings, too.

Mace

Unbearable it is, to be a creature thus changed. To end their lives, mercy it sometimes is. —Yoda

Krespuckle the Ever-Hungry, my favored Leviathan

troops from Endymion. I will not allow the Jedi to eliminate us by assaulting a secure fortification in overwhelming numbers. The Sith will not repeat the mistakes of Bothawui.

## RIM CAMPAIGN — DAY 133 — MALGUS

Despite our setback, the will of my army remains strong. We have been deployed to Ord Radama. Our bivouac is secure, and I have a moment of quiet.

We arrived here four days ago. The dropships touched down under heavy fire, and I led the disembarkation alongside Darth Venemal. Our lightsabers provided a sufficient screen for the single file lines of infantry behind us. We charged the heavy guns embedded in the cliff face, and they roared to life in response. *Those who can touch the dark side have sight where others are blind. They*

When both transports exploded at our backs, I knew the Republic's gunners had chosen the wrong targets. We had *must always* several critical seconds before they could ready another *lead those* shot. By that time, we had reached the cover of the rocks *who lack* at the cliff's base. Had they fired at the two Sith Lords *that ability.* leading the way, our assault would have ended there. Not even I can deflect a cannon burst from a Merr-Sonn Bellower.

I ordered Lord Venemal to leap onto the shelf from which the cannon barrels protruded. Moments later, the machinery fell silent and he signaled the all clear. The commandos fired their ascension hooks and joined him on top.

Leading the remaining troops up the mountain trail, a tremor in the Force echoed through me. The defenders of Ord Radama had placed mines on the path. Enraged by such cowardice, I hurled a boulder from the mountainside onto the path in front of us. I then slowly rolled it twenty paces ahead of our own progress, using focused mental energy channeled through the dark side. The stone detonated each

of the mines and scattered a nest of ambushers. <u>My fire troopers</u>
<u>took care of them with the spray of their flamethrower.</u>

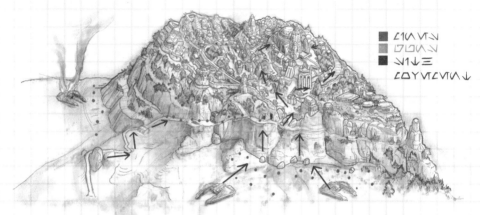

**Our ascent on Ord Radama exploited the natural cover offered by the ridge.**

We rejoined Venemal's team at the mountain's crest. His
commandos had swept the Republic stronghold, leaving
no survivors. I had to congratulate their thoroughness.

Our communications officer signaled the Lindworm,
and the rest of our troops landed on the field we had just
secured. From start to finish, we lost only two dropships
and their crews.

This evening, as my soldiers readied their gear, I
summoned them to bolster their spirits. Standing atop a
siege tank, my mighty call echoed for kilometers:

"YOU ARE SERVANTS OF THE EMPEROR AND OF THE
EMPIRE! YOU ARE THE ENGINE OF CONFLICT. YOU ARE
TRANSFORMING THE GALAXY!"

The soldiers raised their weapons and their voices in
agreement. Our progress has been swift. We will soon
take the capital city of Livien Magnus.

ACCORDING TO HISTORY, DARTH MALGUS LATER PARTICIPATED IN THE SACKING OF CORUSCANT AND NEARLY DESTROYED THE JEDI TEMPLE. BECAUSE THE SITH ARE NEVER AT PEACE, THEY ALWAYS SEEK TO HARM OTHERS. —LUKE

The capital city of Livien Magnus has fallen. I have brought glory to the Empire, but my satisfaction was cut short by the arrival of Lord Adraas.

Lord Adraas arrived two days ago, sent by the Dark Council to assist in our operations. His presence and the Council's decision anger me. Our siege of Livien Magnus had only been in effect a week, hardly enough time to declare it a stalemate. The city would have fallen when its people starved. Was that not the strategy behind the Mandalorian Blockade, which the Dark Council orchestrated? The tactic choked traffic along the Hydian Way and made our current campaign possible. Yet, the Council dares to hint that I lack courage.

Worse still is Adraas's smirking confidence during our strategy sessions. How I hate that weakling, who seeks his own advancement over the goals of the Sith Empire. Adraas brought ten platoons of war droids, roughly half of them Mark I models and the other half Mark IIs. Adraas is confident these droids can blast through the city's perimeter defenses and clear a path to the shield generator that is covering the city in a protective energy canopy. I do not disabuse him of this notion.

*I do not care for war droids. I find them useful only as lightsaber training opponents. —Vader*

I know Mark I war droids are well armed, with rapid-fire twin blasters attached to each arm. Mark II droids have similar weaponry and better armor—but neither model is nimble. The Colicoid insects that built them installed a pointy-legged, shuffling locomotion system that leaves them vulnerable to flanking maneuvers. Venemal and I have both witnessed this weakness.

Sith war droids, Mark I and Mark II models

*There is some truth to this. Droids are throwaway soldiers, easy to build and effective only when unleashed in overwhelming numbers.*

So with a small nod toward Lord Venemal, we agreed with Lord Adraas as he announced his intention to stage an assault on the southern gate. We watched as the war droids were sent into battle and were chewed to shrapnel in the crossfire of the Republic's entrenched infantry.

But the failure did provide a distraction. With the enemy's attention focused elsewhere, Lord Venemal led his commandos over the western wall and blasted a hole from the inside out, enabling the rest of our troops to pour into the city.

We shut down the shield generator in less than an hour. I then called in air support to shatter all remaining pockets of resistance.

Should it surprise me that Lord Adraas claimed credit for the victory when he reported the news to Darth Angral? No, I am not surprised. I am disgusted.

Adraas—oblivious to our strategizing

## RIM CAMPAIGN — DAY 179 — MALGUS

We will lose Ord Radama if we are not resupplied. That fool Adraas is gone, slinking back to Dromund Kaas to curry favor with the Dark Council. Meanwhile, Lord Venemal and I are left here to carry on our work, defending the city from agitators. Our numbers steadily dwindle.

The essential quality of the Force is conflict. Through conflict, the strong kill the weak and bring the living closer to perfection. The Sith Empire has served the Force by inciting conflict. But for true improvement to take place, I must at least give my soldiers a fighting chance against the enemies who seek to destroy them.

The Ministry of Logistics is responsible for our resupply, but my influence with Minister Khamarr has never been strong. She is a favorite of the Dark Council and rewards the needs of Dromund Kaas above all others. I, instead, have sent my requests to War Minister Shareis but have received no answer.

Politics sicken me. Begging for resources from a bureaucrat is not a fitting role for a Sith Lord. All such functionaries should be honored to do my bidding and should scramble to see it done. For we Sith Lords are elevated above the non-Force users who staff our galactic regime. But neither Minister Shareis nor his Grand Moffs can do anything for me if other Sith Lords have already placed claims on his resources.

The glow lantern on the ration crate has dimmed to nearly nothing as I write these words. The rattling bursts of the cacophanizer shells have quieted into a far-off rumble. I think of you, Eleena. As ever, the rage within me ignites when I think of how you have been kept from me.

My Eleena

All aliens are slaves under the Sith Empire. Every resource must be exploited when the cause is total victory. But you, Eleena, have proven yourself—as a servant and as a fighter, and perhaps as something more. When I have achieved all I envision, I will have any companion I wish. Not even the Emperor would dare command otherwise.

*Attachment such as this leads to loss and tragedy. I have tried to learn more, but the journals of Darth Malgus do not reveal the fate of his secret love.* —Vader

# RIM CAMPAIGN — DAY 215 — MALGUS

Disaster. We have abandoned Ord Radama. Venemal is dead and so is the legion of troops under my command.

My resupplies never arrived. No doubt Minister Shareis felt Lord Adraas, or some other dilettante, should be well armed for another needless inspection tour. Through his incompetence, the Empire is losing its hold on the systems we have only just secured.

Imbeciles, all of them.

I hear that even the Mandalorian Blockade is crumbling, because of the two smugglers allied with the Republic. If the Hydian Way is reopened, the trickle of Republic reinforcements that retook Ord Radama will become a flood.

The Battle of Ord Radama was not lost on the ground. Venemal and I could have held the capital city indefinitely, armed with only our lightsabers. But in orbit overhead, we had only the dreadnought Lindworm and <u>two Harrower battle cruisers</u>.

In opposition, four Republic Hammerhead-class cruisers and ten Thranta-class corvettes dropped from hyperspace. They broadsided the Lindworm with a turbolaser barrage before she could launch her starfighters.

From the balcony of the palace in Livien Magnus, I saw the flashes of orbital combat as the comm erupted with static and anxious chatter. I boarded my shuttle, ordering Captain Karm to take me up to the Lindworm, where I could assume command.

The captain performed with characteristic skill, evading the Republic's Aurek fighters and making a hard landing in the Lindworm's ventral bay. But by the time the turbolift got me to the bridge, I could see the battle was lost.

*Imperial Star Destroyers are similar to Harrowers and shall be my tools of discipline among the rebellious systems of the Rim.*

THE REBELS RELIED ON PINPOINT HYPERSPACE JUMPS TO AMBUSH THE IMPERIAL FLEET.

IN SOME WAYS, DECISIONS ARE SIMPLER WHEN YOU'RE OUTNUMBERED AND OUTGUNNED.

—LUKE

One of our Harrowers gushed flames as it let loose a rain of escape pods. The other Harrower lay fatally stricken, its guts torn loose by a cluster of proton torpedoes. I could do nothing to halt its fall into Ord Radama's gravitational pull. Minutes later, it impacted at the center of Livien Magnus.

The wounded Harrower begins its descent.

At that instant, I felt Venemal and a hundred thousand other life-forms roar with pain and then fall silent. *Through the Force,*

The strength of my scream buckled the bridge's *anguish can carry* transparisteel viewport and left the crew's ears bleeding. *great* More gratifyingly, my rage overloaded the fuel slugs of an *power.* incoming wave of Aureks. The bright bursts of their deaths *Vader* raised a smile.

Nothing could be gained by remaining in the star system. I ordered the dazed navigator to maneuver the Lindworm behind the ion minefield and to make the jump into the heart of Sith Space.

The Republic pursued us. The Mandalorian Blockade has now fully crumbled. The enemy fleet has penetrated Imperial space.

The Republic made a strike at Korriban, though they have threatened that world far too many times for me to consider it their true target. So it was expected when their fleet jumped, but it is now gathered before Ziost.

Our situation is dire, and victory hinges on space superiority. The Republic's capital ships have not broken our defensive line, but their small starfighters have easily slipped through our screen. The Battle of Ziost will be won by the pilots.

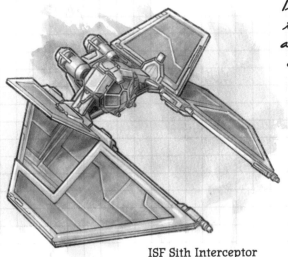

*Interesting that ship to-ship combat played a critical role even then. Starfighters can outmaneuver capital ships and exploit their weaknesses.*

*Vader*

THE REBELLION USED THE SAME STRATEGY. THE EMPIRE OUTNUMBERED US, BUT WE HAD BETTER PILOTS.

—LUKE

ISF Sith Interceptor

Daily skirmishes take place in orbit and in the atmosphere. And each time, a few of the Republic's fastest interceptors and heavy bombers make it through our defenses to the treetops of Ziost. We have lost vital cannon batteries and weapon arsenals.

Our only protection against this aggression is the skill of our Imperial pilots and the superior technology of our

*The role of these interceptors is comparable to the Empire's TIE fighters. Many design elements are the same.*

*Vader*

starfighters. Our ISF interceptors are lightweight and maneuverable. But though the interceptors are optimal for high-speed dogfighting, our B-28 starfighters fill the firepower gap with their heavy armament. Our Fury-class interceptors act as heavy transports, patrolling the borders of the fray to pick off any ship that tries to make a break for the surface.

Darth Angral believes we are evenly matched with the Republic, and that we have arrived at an impasse. He is requisitioning more naval vessels from Dromund Kaas. I have urged caution. A Jedi commander skilled in battle meditation could link warships and starfighters into a single mind, and the Jedi have other tricks that could turn the tide in their favor.

*HEARING ABOUT THESE OLD MODELS IS FASCINATING. AS FAR AS I KNOW, NO FLYABLE RELICS STILL EXIST. TOO BAD, BECAUSE I'D LOVE TO PUT ONE THROUGH ITS PACES.*

*—LUKE*

## RIM CAMPAIGN — DAY 258 — MALGUS

We must now defend the heart of our own territory. I am enraged the Dark Council allowed the war to reach Ashas Ree, yet I must allow some measure of admiration for the way the Republic has outmaneuvered us.

They made their first strike while Lord Angral's vessels were still gathered at Ziost. We arrived just in time to halt their advance on the central garrison. Do they think they can hold this world? Do they hope to fortify it as a staging point for a strike against Dromund Kaas? Or is this a way to preoccupy our forces yet again, while they capture some other objective?

*The capital of any fighting force must be protected above all else. An army that loses the capital, loses its authority.*

*Coruscant is impenetrable. No enemy can ever hope to shake my hold on this world.*

*Vader*

*IT WAS YEARS BEFORE THE NEW REPUBLIC FINALLY TOOK CORUSCANT FROM PALPATINE'S SUCCESSORS, BUT PERSEVERANCE PAYS OFF.*

*—LUKE*

I write from a clearing at the garrison's outskirts, amid the encampments of the planet's doctrinists, who desire a return to the Empire's isolationism. They have often stood in opposition to our Emperor—but today, we are all Sith.

**Sith siege tanks at the shield's edge**

I command a line of siege tanks positioned to hold off the Republic's armored floaters that regularly prod our defenses along the jungle border. Above my head, the energy shield protecting the garrison flares white with each impact of a mortar shell. Occasionally, a thundering turbolaser blast reaches us from the naval clash in orbit.

I have learned that the Republic commander behind this bold move is Jedi Master Ven Zallow. Despite his allegiance to Jedi blasphemy, he at least appears to grasp the truth of improvement through combat.

Master Zallow, and those like him, may yet realize their errors and join the Sith cause. Until then, I will do everything in my power to rid the galaxy of them. Ever since my vision at Korriban those many years ago, I have known that my destiny is to exterminate the Jedi and topple their obscene Temple.

*The Jedi Temple needed to be destroyed if we hoped to end the Clone Wars. In the end I saved lives.* Vader

# RIM CAMPAIGN — DAY 315 — MALGUS

The Battle of Ashas Ree is over—another victory for the Empire! And once again, the unworthy have sought status in the wake of this triumph. Adraas is nothing but a vile rootworm feeding on the carcasses of the beasts I slay. One day I will no longer tolerate his antics. I will make him suffer.

The Dark Council recognized the role I played in the *I do not respect spies and others who hide in shadows.* planet's defense and has informed me, through one of its agents, that I will not again experience a materiel shortage *Those who wish to* like the one that cost us Ord Radama. The Council's approval *fight should* is meaningless, but I will gladly accept its resources. *make their intentions clear.*

I received word from Imperial Intelligence that Jedi Master *Vader* Ven Zallow and his forces are headquartered on Serenno. That ancient world of noble houses would react too swiftly to a direct assault, so <u>I have activated an infiltrator.</u>

The Emperor, in his wisdom, spent many decades installing Sith infiltrators in positions of power across the galaxy—long before our armada fired its first shot. Indeed, these agents turned the governments of Ruuria, Sernpidal, and Belkadan to our cause. Their devious work allowed for the ambush of the Republic fleet in the Tingel Arm—our first major victory in this war.

Only a fraction of the Emperor's infiltrators have been activated to date. But Darth Caba has gathered intelligence reports, which indicate a high-ranking Serenno noble, who has the ear of Master Zallow, is secretly one of ours.

Ven Zallow is blind to the threat in his own command center.

*Serenno's importance has gone undiminished by time. My servant, Count Dooku, rallied Separatist systems by exploiting his status as a Serenno noble.*

59

There is urgency to this situation, however. Information provided by high-ranking agents—ciphers, they call themselves—suggests the Republic may soon move from Serenno to a new forward base. If we do not strike now, we will lose our moment.

The assassination of Master Zallow and the disruption of the Republic's command structure must be carried out. But I have been told I must wait for one of the infiltrators to complete the mission. And so we wait for word of success to come through the cipher network.

My warships stand ready. I will not eat, drink, or sleep until we have joined battle. Denial quickens the senses and sharpens the mind. I must be in top form, for Serenno is crawling with Jedi. TRANSPARENCY IS ONE OF THE PRINCIPLES OF THE NEW REPUBLIC THAT I CONTINUE TO CHAMPION. THE PEOPLE HAVE A RIGHT TO KNOW WHAT THEIR LEADERS KNOW. I'VE ARGUED THIS

# RIM CAMPAIGN — DAY 342 — MALGUS  POINT A HUNDRED TIMES WITH CHIEF OF STATE FEY'LYA.

The operation on Serenno only partially succeeded. A    —LUKE subspace transmission from the ciphers announced that the infiltrator had struck. I ordered the fleet to make the leap. We surprised the Republic vessels and scattered them.

We secured House Palerma's villa, which the Jedi had been using as a command post. But rage tore through me when I discovered the infiltrator's body lying in the banquet hall, cut in two by Zallow's lightsaber. And Zallow had escaped aboard one of the Republic cruisers!

Although Serenno now belongs to the Empire, it does not accept us. Incredibly, the Houses of Teramo and Comprassi have hired mercenaries to evict us. I awoke last night to the sound of magnetic accelerator shells punching through the permacrete plaster of the villa's walls.

Fortunately, I came to Serenno prepared. The Dark Council supplied me with a squad of elite assassins. I have never desired their path. My power comes from fury, honed by combat. I prefer to smell the fear in an enemy's sweat rather than manipulate him with spells from afar. But at that moment, I was glad to have the assassins under my command.

**Sith assassins complete their sweep of the grounds.**

From a parapet, I watched the assassins ring the villa and fan out in all directions. They lit up the moonless dark with blue flashes of lightning. Their commanders directed them toward the attackers, like battle neks pursuing a hunting quarry.

The mercenaries abandoned their heavy weapons and fired back with antiquated pulse-wave pistols. A pathetic attempt with feeble weapons. Their screams soon ceased, and I secured a few more hours of sleep before sunrise.

## RIM CAMPAIGN — DAY 399 — MALGUS

The Sith Emperor has ordered us to recapture Ord Radama. I will lead the attack. There are rumors that some blame me for the death of Lord Venemal and the defeat we suffered there. This campaign shall restore my honor and prove the fitness of the Sith Empire.

I am leaving nothing to chance. Typical soldiers do not use the dark side, and Sith Inquisitors are too hands-off for my tastes. For this battle, I will command a regiment of Force-strong warriors.

The methods and traditions of the warrior are my own. From my father's meditations on death to the lessons of my tutors in the Dromund Kaas academy, I was nurtured by the dark side and grew strong. Others dull their senses with spice and drink, but warriors know that combat is the only experience to be savored.

Other Sith Lords keep their elite dark side warriors in reserve, far from the enemy, to preserve their strategic insights. What a waste! They have attained their rank because they have fought and won. To deny them the honor of combat is to call them useless. Not only is it an insult, it weakens the Sith Empire as a whole.

*Warriors are animals. Agents like Darth Maul have their uses, but can never expand beyond their limited set of tasks.*

A Sith warrior embodies purity.

I will lead the assault on Ord Radama's relocated capital city of New Raido. My warriors are experts in the art of wielding two lightsabers and are outfitted with combat armor newly manufactured on Balmorra. The armor is heavy, but warriors are capable of endless endurance.

*It is true there is honor in one-on-one combat.*

Droids, troopers, commandos, and more will follow after we breach the city's defenses. Imperial Intelligence reports that the Republic has done little to fortify Ord Radama, and the natives have struggled to survive following the destruction of Livien Magnus.

*I grow tired of the backstabbing of Imperial bureaucrats. —Vader*

62

Our victory will hardly qualify as a conflict, but it will be enough. From Ord Radama, I will be able to seek new targets of conquest for the improvement of the Sith Empire. FEEDING ON RAGE LIKE THIS BRINGS FIGHTERS TO THE DARK SIDE, BUT WHEN THEY STEP AWAY THEY CAN BE

## RIM CAMPAIGN — DAY 460 — MALGUS MUCH MORE RECEPTIVE TO THE LIGHT. NOT ALL SUCH WARRIORS

The Reconquest of Ord Radama is entering its 51st day. ARE BEYOND REDEMPTION. A different commander would feel dismay at our loss of life —LUKE or at the way the Jedi confounded Intelligence's ciphers by remaining in disguise amid the planet's peasantry until we had launched our attack. Not I. This is exhilaration. An easy conquest would count for little, but this glorious bloodbath benefits both sides.

The Jedi have always been our true targets, not the Republic's lowly troopers or the ragged insurgents of subjugated worlds. Now we have lightsaber combat and Force dueling on a grand scale. With each corpse we create, we expose the lie of their offensive pacifism. Those who perish in our own ranks are like knots shaved from a stake of greel wood. We grow sharper with each slice of the knife.

The pace of this battle has cost me favor with the Dark Council and Darth Angral. But I will emerge victorious, and my triumph will ensure my place in the army that strikes Coruscant.

Many Jedi died in the glorious bloodbath of Ord Radama.

THE EMPEROR'S LOVE OF SUPERWEAPONS HELPED US DEFEAT HIM.

A BIG WEAPON IS ALSO A BIG TARGET, AND NOTHING IS INVINCIBLE. —LUKE

**The core mechanism of the Dark Reaper as recorded in the Qel-Droma Holocron**

This battle will not last much longer. During the last Great Sith War, the Dark Lord Exar Kun built a weapon of such <u>power it could rip the life essence from an entire army</u>. It was known as the Dark Reaper. Although it has been lost to time, the Dark Council believes its core mechanism is somewhere on Ord Radama.

*A spark of insight from Malgus. A Sith should always think on a monumental scale.*

Just as we shall soon taste victory, we shall also soon discover this weapon. I do not care whether we deploy it here or on Coruscant. I serve the Emperor by cutting away the unworthy. Let there be no mercy for the Jedi.

## RIM CAMPAIGN — DAY 479 — MALGUS

*This weapon was unearthed on Raxus Prime during the Clone Wars. Malgus was digging in the wrong place. Vader*

I am assembling a task force to stage a Coreward assault on Republic space. The Dark Council has placed the following assets at my disposal:

- 4 Harrower battle cruisers
- 48 Fury-class transports
- 192 ISF interceptors
- 720 Mark I war droids
- 480 Mark II war droids

64

# THE RULE
## OF TWO

# POWER OF THE SITH

*The Force is not fire, it is venom.*

In that simple maxim is the entirety of Sith philosophy. What Lord Kaan and my other, lesser predecessors could not understand is that such a fundamental truth is not evidence of insight on my part but, rather, stupidity on their part.

The Force is not fire. It cannot be passed from one user's lit torch to another's, and another's, until an entire hemisphere is illuminated with a blaze of a million lights. This is what Kaan foolishly believed, and all Sith Lords before him for the past thousand years. It is why the once mighty Sith fell apart long before the defeat at Ruusan. When all carry a flame, no matter how dim and guttering it may be, they soon conclude they are the brightest stars, around which all others must orbit. Infighting follows, and Jedi victory becomes inevitable.

No, the Force is venom. If it is poured into many cups, it loses its potency until it becomes so diluted it is merely an irritant. Yet pour those cups back into a single vessel and you will have the power to stop a Krayt dragon's heart.

This is the secret. This is the Rule of Two: One Sith must contain all the power of the dark side. One Master must decide how that power shall be used. Sharing power is an act of weakness and a violation of the Sith Code.

BANE WAS WRONG. THE FORCE IS FIRE. WHEN THE EMPEROR HELD POWER, THE JEDI WERE NEARLY EXTINGUISHED AND THE GALAXY SUFFERED. I HAVE WORKED TO RESTORE THE JEDI ORDER, AND WE GROW STRONGER AS WE PASS THE FLAME—OUR LIGHT SPREADS. —LUKE

THE LINK FROM MASTER TO PUPIL IS THE UNDERPINNING OF OUR ORDER.

Yet, the Sith Order *must* survive after the Master perishes. For this reason, the Master must take an apprentice. The Master instructs the pupil but never gives up the smallest sliver of power. The apprentice learns through years of study but must struggle for every achievement. If the apprentice becomes strong enough, a battle to the death will prove it. If the Master should be struck down, the apprentice becomes the Master—and the Order continues.

Together the two may attract legions of minions, but true power will remain concentrated. Always two—a Master and an apprentice.

*Bane's power has been passed down for a thousand years. I vow to be its last recipient.*

# THE MISTAKES OF RUUSAN

"All are equal in the Brotherhood of Darkness." Those putrid words fell from the lips of Lord Kaan more times than I care to remember. This central lie, upon which Kaan built his false Sith, is the reason behind their watery, diluted power.

The so-called New Sith Wars lasted a thousand years. Many warlords during that time sought to control the destiny of the Sith Empire. They achieved victories from the Battle of Mizra to the Sictus Wars, but those were victories without a clear line of succession. Every Sith wanted to be king. And so we argued, while the Republic grew frail—its citizens sickened with plague—and became isolated by a decaying infrastructure. Coruscant's throat lay bare beneath our blades, but the Sith plunged their knives into one another's backs instead! Kaan was not the worst of these fools, only the last.

Kaan created the Brotherhood of Darkness to end this squabbling, but he chose a false egalitarianism over a strong central rule. Within the Brotherhood, all members with rank called themselves Sith Lords. This was Kaan's first mistake.

I served in the Brotherhood of Darkness as a sergeant assigned to the Gloom Walkers and led my comrades in the capture of Phaseem. If we had maintained a sound military strategy and followed an orderly conquest, the Republic would have been ours. But Kaan was impatient. He overreached and leaped into the Bormea sector, the Republic's heart, before it was time. This was his second mistake.

Kaan's third and final mistake came at Ruusan, a worthless world where he hoped to defeat Lord Hoth and the Jedi Army of Light. He was instead goaded into a grinding land war of

*Qvos*

*I've heard of the Ruusan Reformations, but didn't know all this. Why don't the Jedi talk about this battle?*

KAAN AND HIS LACKIES—NONE OF THEM KNEW THEIR PLACE.

THE THOUGHT BOMB AT RUUSAN

needless attrition. I watched it unfold and knew the Sith had become like the Jedi—too numerous and too weak. Kaan had lost his grip.

In the end, Kaan followed my suggestion and pooled the abilities of the other Sith Lords to create a brute-force wonder: the thought bomb. This was proof of what the dark side could achieve when it wasn't split among thousands. However, the thought bomb consumed not only the Jedi combatants but also the Sith who had created it. It ended the war and exterminated Lord Kaan's Brotherhood.

KYLE KATARN, ONE OF MY STUDENTS, UNFOLDED THE THOUGHT BOMB'S VORTEX AT RUUSAN AND FREED THE SPIRITS THAT HAD BEEN TRAPPED INSIDE FOR MORE THAN A THOUSAND YEARS.

—LUKE

# The Title of Darth

If my plan had not worked and Kaan had not killed himself with the thought bomb, I would have been forced to kill him myself. The annihilation at Ruusan was a gift, wiping out all those who were not worthy. I, Darth Bane, and my apprentice, Darth Zannah, survived and returned the potency of the Sith to our hands, so the Rule of Two could be instituted.

It is no accident that I took the title of Darth when I gained a mastery of the dark side, nor is it an accident that Kaan and his followers rejected it. It is a title of power. It carries authority and is crowned by the judgment of history. It symbolizes transformation. When I took Darth as my title, I put away my childhood name. What does it matter that I was once a miner or a soldier? The only thing that matters is what I will achieve.

Andeddu, Revan, Malak, Malgus, Ruin—their line culminates with me.

Some believe the *Darth* itself is derived from the ancient Rakatan term *darr tah*, meaning "triumph over death," or *daritha*, meaning "emperor." But the word's true meaning does not come from any language but from the proud histories and accomplishments of those who have borne the title:

Darth Andeddu, the god-king of Prakith, who sought to live forever.

Darth Revan and Darth Malak, who built a new Sith Empire that rivaled the Republic in its influence across the galaxy.

Darth Malgus, who led his troops into the Jedi Temple during the Sacking of Coruscant.

Darth Ruin, who left the Jedi Order to pursue his monomaniacal philosophy of self-interest and gave rise to the thousand-year war that concluded at Ruusan, and who was among the last to hold the Darth title—until I took it up again.

Lord Kaan preached that all were equal in the Brotherhood of Darkness, but he did not dare to appoint a thousand Darths. In fact, he did not permit the use of the title at all. Perhaps he sensed its inherent power—that an individual who held the title would not allow rivals to live. Perhaps its use would have forced Kaan to confront the truth—that his approach to the Force was a disgrace.

I restored the title of Darth to the Rule of Two so that only the worthy may hold it from this time, until the end of time.

THE TITLE SEEMS TO HAVE EXPIRED WITH MY FATHER. I'M PROUD IT WAS MY FAMILY THAT FINALLY PUT AN END TO IT.

—LUKE

Darth Maul, Darth Tyranus, Darth Vader. Each useful in his own way. Each easy to replace when his purpose has reached its end.

72

*I have struck from the shadows while remaining in plain view. It is a superior disguise.*

# STRIKING FROM THE SHADOWS

The Sith of old brazenly and publicly announced their superiority. In this, they were correct. They were mistaken, though, if they thought no legion of enemies would rise up against them.

The Sith have always been smeared as wicked, evil beings, no different from the cacodemons of children's tales who lurk in dark places with dripping fangs. Because submission to such horror is unthinkable, many believe they must fight or face extermination. The Jedi are shameless in spreading this alarmist propaganda.

Under the Rule of Two, the Sith will operate in secrecy—feeding the belief that the Sith are a thing of the past, forgotten in their graves on Ruusan. We must not make our presence known.

The dark side of the Force is finally concentrated. It gives the two beings unlimited power, but the Sith cannot afford the loss of either of you! Do not make yourselves targets. Even a Sith Lord can be felled by a thousand enemies.

If there exists a single being who believes in the continued existence of the Sith, kill him. If a group learns the secret, you must resort to subterfuge and misdirection. At one point, the Jedi believed they had evidence of my own survival after Ruusan. My apprentice and I concocted a ruse in which she drove her brother insane and made him appear to be the terrible "Sith Lord." This satisfied the Jedi need to assign blame, and they moved on.

This tendency to hide worries me. There may be threats out there that we haven't encountered yet. —LUKE

The Jedi learned about the Rule of Two more than a century ago from the cultist Kibh Jeen. Some of them didn't believe it. Now that Obi-Wan's fight on Naboo has confirmed the truth, the Jedi are ready to face whatever the Sith have been cooking up. QVos

73

THE MASTERMINDS OF THE UNDERWORLD ARE MERELY PUPPETS OF THE SITH.

The Sith Order is now a lineage. Given your skills, you should find it a simple matter to amass wealth, and thus with each succession the resources of the Sith will increase. Do not build palaces, for they will draw attention. Use your money to hire spies, scholars, assassins, trainers, guards, and thieves. All will prove useful, and the shine of credits will distract them from your true nature.

Curious. I have brought the Sith to their ultimate victory. Through study, I will soon learn how to defeat death. While I may choose apprentices, I will never choose a successor.

# SELECTING AN APPRENTICE

**A**gain, the Sith Order is a lineage. *It must not end with you!* I will not allow my new Sith Order to expire because you were unworthy or too protective to bequeath your power.

Know this: Your apprentice will kill you. If this fact frightens you, then the Sith Order has already suffered a fatal infection. Your existence in the Order is not needed. Your battle has already been lost.

A Sith apprentice must grow in strength and skill until he or she can surpass the Master. Anything else is regression! Would you have the Sith become like the "kings" of Shawken whose dominion crumbled into ruin?

Or do you believe you will live forever? You are not wrong to covet that secret, for I have sought to prolong my own life. But in the extreme, this leads to narcissism and a lack of focus on the Rule of Two. To be a Sith Lord is to outthink your enemies and to plan for any eventuality. A proper apprentice will ensure that the Sith endure, no matter what fate may come upon your head.

Many Force-sensitive beings exist among the stars. Seek out those who have not yet been discovered or subjected to Jedi corruption. You will find it easier to mold the young, for their bodies and minds are still in flux. You may wish to train several candidates at once. Their rivalries will force their essential natures to the surface, making it unlikely they will join forces against you.

Tell them only one will survive to become your apprentice. Let them defeat one another in combat, betray one another in their sleep, or play with one's suspicions and tensions. All are

THIS IS THE REASON WHY THE JEDI ENCOURAGE TRAINING FROM CHILDHOOD. As their powers grow, those who can use the Force must learn how they can help OTHERS, not merely themselves. —LUKE

admirable skills for a future Sith Lord. Then watch as they destroy one another.

I did not have the luxury of employing this method when selecting my own apprentice. But if she should prove reluctant to take my place, I will train a second apprentice to replace her. The talented and the ambitious will receive their reward, the rest will taste only ashes.

CONFLICT SHARPENS ONE'S SKILLS AND MAKES THE SITH STRONGER.

# The Revenge of the Sith

Under the Rule of Two, the Sith will concentrate power in one Master and one apprentice so that one day we will reveal ourselves to the Jedi. Eventually, we will have revenge.

Galactic civilization is an empty term when that civilization lacks leadership. Given a clear vision and the means to enact it, a Sith regime could build great wonders in defiance of the natural laws of silence, stillness, and ruin. Kaan was a fool, but he was right in one thing: the laws of the current Republic only abet these chaotic forces, and only the Sith way leads to mastery over entropy.

I HAVE BEHELD A GALAXY UNDER SITH RULE.

The Jedi path teaches harmony and peace. But if all we aspired to was harmony, then intelligent beings would still be scratching for food from rotted tree stumps. The dark side of the Force is both an enabler and a guide. To advance the cause of the Sith, you must fight those who would hold back progress. You, and those who succeed you, are building an arsenal of dark side potency. One day it will contain the power to destroy the Jedi and bring purpose to the Force.

Remember the Code of the Sith: *There is no peace, only passion.* In creating a new regime, the Sith will defeat the complacency of the Jedi. And what we create will be glorious!

# PERSONAL COMBAT

I have stated that the Force is venom. Because you are a Sith Lord, you realize the truth in my words. You cannot dilute our power! You must also keep yourself strong, not only in numbers but in combat. The purest expression of victory is through combat. I will not permit my legacy to become a blurred copy of a copy. These pages contain what you must know if you wish to defeat an enemy with a lightsaber or the Force. Do not rely solely on what your own Master has taught you. Study these arts, drink directly from the source.

# Lightsaber Construction

The lightsaber is the weapon of a Sith Lord. Properly wielded, it is an extension of your body, a limb that requires no conscious thought to move or position. If you lose your lightsaber, it should feel as if you have suffered an amputation. *I'd love to have an edge in combat, but this is wishful thinking by the Sith. Red blades are weaker and THEY'RE the ones that*

The Jedi also carry lightsabers. They harvest their lightsaber *break. Jedi* crystals from a mine. The Sith, however, have long had a *don't like artificial* superior alternative. Raw elements cooked in a brood furnace *crystals* will produce an artificial crystal—one that can generate an *anyway,* energy blade that will burn with a bright crimson light. *not when there are such beauties on Ilum.* —Q vos

REMOVING THE DROSS FROM A FORGED SITH CRYSTAL

*This is what has become of the Jedi—watered down and weak.*

Because this artificial crystal is forged through dark side mediation, it carries the essence of your will. Know that your red blade is strong and can break the green and blue blades of a Jedi! Such results are proof that an individual can overcome anything found in nature.

*THE LIGHTSABER IS A MECHANICAL CONSTRUCT, BUT I BELIEVE THAT THE USE OF A NATURAL CRYSTAL HELPS LINK IT TO THE LIVING FORCE.*

*—LUKE*

# Sith Lightsaber Variants

The remaining components of the lightsaber can be assembled from everyday materials or the rarest of metals. It matters little, so long as the crystalline heart has been forged by your will. The other elements—a power cell, an emitter matrix, and a magnetic emitter ring or focusing lens—will be placed around the red shard within the hilt. The crystal is special, but these pieces are replaceable. Use them, replace them, but always ensure that the crystal and the blade are bright and strong.

Depending on your chosen fighting style, you may incorporate innovations in your lightsaber hilt that will aid you. You should not care for ceremony, only for results. If an innovation works, do not hesitate to use it. If it proves superfluous, remove it immediately.

**Blade lock:** A small notch added next to the activation stud will make it possible to leave the blade extended after it leaves your hand. This is useful for throwing, but can prove dangerous if the lightsaber is jarred out of your hands or buffeted with a Force push.

LOCKING THE BLADE INTO POSITION WILL TURN YOUR LIGHTSABER INTO A JAVELIN.

These hilt variations are interesting. Streen, one of my former students, built a hidden compartment in his lightsaber to hold New Republic credit chips.

—Luke

**Pressure grip:** This customization replaces an activation stud and assures that the lightsaber will ignite only when held. If you align the pressure grip to your unique biology, you will be the only one who can activate it.

**Force activation:** With this configuration, the circuit that connects the power cell to the crystal can only be completed with your mental energy. Only you can wield such a lightsaber. But if your attention lags during combat, the blade may blink off.

**Beskar hilt:** Beskar, also known as Mandalorian iron, is resistant to a lightsaber blow. This material is extremely rare, but if you choose to incorporate it into your hilt design, it could be used to intercept a Jedi blade.

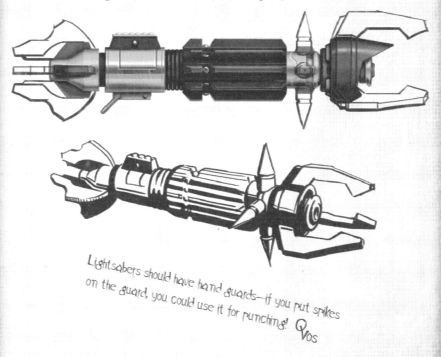

Lightsabers should have hand guards—if you put spikes on the guard, you could use it for punching! —Quos

# LIGHTSABER COMBAT

The Jedi teach six forms of lightsaber combat. This is excessive and a waste of time. There is no need for a Sith Lord to study any form that does not channel one's aggression. A battle should end quickly. At every moment, one should be assessing the ways to dispatch one's opponent—select the most direct method.

There are two key forms of lightsaber combat a Sith must master: Strong style and Fast style. The latter emphasizes footwork, speed, precision, and acrobatics. With some exceptions—such as the tactics of my own apprentice—Fast style is rarely suited for a Sith. The dark side supplies us with strength, and that strength must be used. Hate makes us powerful.

Strong style is expressed as *djem so*—an ancient philosophy that requires you to combine your body weight and your

STRONG STYLE IS ONLY SUITABLE FOR THE POWERFUL.

muscular strength with the energizing drug of anger so that the execution of your blows will land with enough force to crack armor.

muscular strength with the energizing drug of anger so that the execution of your blows will land with enough force to crack armor.

When used for defense, *djem so* turns an attack back on the attacker. If you deflect a blade at a vulnerable angle, it will draw your opponent in <u>close enough for a gutting slash or an elbow to the face.</u> Deflecting a blow may also draw your enemy into a blade lock, which is easily won with the strength of your arms and the power of your hate.

Another facet of Strong style defense is *shien*, or blocking incoming blaster fire. When generating this defense, some choose to use a reverse grip on the lightsaber hilt. Sith *shien* should be a temporary measure—used only long enough to shorten the blade distance to your opponent or to recover from a kill so that you may find your next target. Deflecting bolts against your attackers can be useful, but be aware that this tactic is a waste of your physical prowess.

Any combat situation or style can be enhanced by the use of *dun möch.* This tactic employs taunts and verbal attacks to weaken your enemy's will. It takes only a few words to expose your opponent's lack of confidence and to lay it out to manipulate.

*My style is a hybrid, but it's built on what I now understand is considered the Jedi Form V. Even the more aggressive Jedi styles emphasize defense, while the Sith only seem to care about attack.* —LUKE

*With the Sith, everything is overkill. There's no need for the killing. When I knock somebody down, they stay down.* Q𝘷ᴏs

*Dun möch may backfire if it provokes an enemy to mindless anger. But rage opens your enemy to the dark side, which can be exploited in its own way.*

There is a third style, though it is exceedingly difficult. It is called *Juyo*—or, as my blademaster obscurely referred to it, Vaapad—and it is a style the Jedi foolishly forbid. The key to this style is the same as our core belief: <u>Emotion, not peace,</u> <u>will lead to victory.</u> With *Juyo*, you must give yourself over to the sensations you feel in the heat of battle: hatred for your enemies; fury toward their actions; and fear that they may prevail. Yes, fear. It is foolish to cover this emotion behind pride. Fear of death, fear of loss, and fear of chaos are primal motivators. Fear can be your fuel.

*Juyo* is based on quick strikes and unpredictable attacks, but you are not fully embracing the style unless your emotions ignite your senses and elevate your abilities. But do not succumb completely to your emotions. You are a Sith Lord, not an animal. As you take aim and fight through the tunnel of rage, you will experience transcendence. In that moment, you are a perfect being and you cannot be beaten—you are at last embraced within *Juyo*.

*JUYO* IS THE MASTERY OF CONTROL, NOT THE LOSS OF IT.

# USING THE SABERSTAFF

The double-bladed lightsaber, or saberstaff, has been known as a Sith weapon since the time of Exar Kun. I studied under the blademaster Kas'im and learned its secrets. It is a difficult weapon.

The saberstaff may be constructed as a single piece, or it may simply be two interlocking saber hilts that can be detached for two-handed combat. It is best used in wide, sweeping movements while the hilt remains close to the body. It requires a firm stance and a two-handed grip. Novices are likely to injure themselves while training, which will expose the flaws in their techniques. Punishment can be a great teacher.

A Sith weapon?
Jedi use these
all the time, like
Master Gelleric
and . . . I guess
that's it. Maybe it
is a Sith weapon. Qvos

THE SABERSTAFF IN ITS LOOSE AND LOCKED CONFIGURATIONS

It IS a Sith weapon, but one suited for the barbarians among us.

Do not be confused into thinking they are two blades. The blades are connected. If you know the position of one, you know the position of the other. But while both blades are in motion, you can choose to extinguish one blade and surprise your enemy with a sword-fighting lunge or riposte.

The saberstaff is ideal for defeating multiple opponents as well as for defending against blaster fire. The broad energy barrier created by a whirling saberstaff is impenetrable when deployed by a skilled Sith Lord—one who possesses the precognitive ability to sense the timing and the vector of a threat. But this type of barrier defense should be used only temporarily, while you close the distance separating you from your attacker to deliver a fatal slash.

IN THE RIGHT HANDS, A SABERSTAFF DOUBLES THE THREAT POSED BY A LIGHTSABER.

Do not feel you must learn everything from your Master, or that you must shoulder the burden of every instruction to your apprentice. The Ailon Nova Guard, the Nikto Morgukai, and the Seyugi Dervishes have all elevated combat into an art form. Hire those who prove useful to your combat education or employ them as assassins or guards. Among their members, look for those who may be touched by the Force—they could become your acolytes or a pool from which to pluck your next apprentice. However, if they learn more of our ways than you are comfortable sharing, kill them.

# Sith Armor

The war against the Jedi birthed great advances in personal combat on both sides. Armorers constantly improved their wares, but lightsaber technology remained constant. By the war's end, a fully armored Jedi Padawan could face a Sith Marauder and survive the first exchange. Donning armor requires understanding two things: how to kill an armored opponent and how to use armor to protect yourself from counterattack. The first comes from combat training. The second requires an understanding of the materials that can withstand a lightsaber blow while still allowing some measure of mobility for the wearer.

If you are accustomed to unarmored sparring, it is best to begin with **armorweave**. This material incorporates a lightweight metallic mesh while maintaining the flexibility of cloth. Armorweave can be arranged to form pieces of fabric armor, or it can be worn as a cloak. It will guard against acids and flame. It can diffuse the energy of blaster bolts, though not their kinetic impact. A lightsaber's point can burn through armorweave, but it will allow you to shrug off glancing blows made with a blade's edge.

**Beskar'kandar** is plate armor cast from Mandalorian iron. Although it is nearly impervious to a lightsaber blade, it is extremely heavy and requires the wearer to rely on a Strong style, or *djem so*, combat stance.

CORTOSIS IS ANOTHER LIGHTSABER COUNTERMEASURE, BUT IN MY EXPERIENCE ARMOR CUTS YOU OFF FROM THE SENSATIONS AND THE AWARENESS OF BATTLE. I VERY MUCH PREFER TO FIGHT UNENCUMBERED. —LUKE

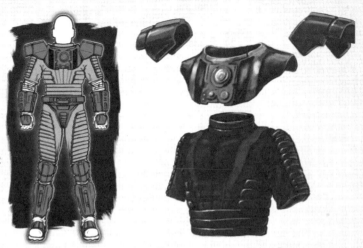

THE DARK ARMOR OF LORD ERADICUS, SQUIRE TO DARTH RUIN

Unique to the Sith is **dark armor**—plate armor that is infused with a dark side essence through Sith alchemy. These suits, once rare, poured from the workshops of Sith armorers during the last war. Many became prizes for battlefield scavengers. Dark armor can almost certainly be found among the black marketeers of the underworld. If one is discovered, it should be reclaimed—and those who seek to profit from our legacy should be eliminated.

The shells of **orbalisks** are quite impervious to lightsabers and can make a fine coat of armor. I myself have tested this bizarre panoply. These parasites breed in the tombs of Dxun. If placed on the skin, they latch on, feeding on Force energy and releasing adrenaline. Once attached, their bodies can almost never be removed.

The protection offered by armor can be augmented with a shield held in your off hand. A shield of polished beskar can also be used as a bashing weapon. Its edges can be honed to razor sharpness and can be used to slice or kill.

Orbalisks torment their hosts with constant agony. A Nikto whom I trained as a dark side adept could not handle the pain. Useless.

89

# Dark Side Combat

You are a Sith Lord, not merely a fighter who knows how to hold a blade. The Force has given you the tools to defeat your enemies. During combat, the dark side crawls beneath your skin and electrifies the air surrounding you. If you fail to channel it during these moments, you are unworthy of the Sith title.

There are three schools, or focuses, of Force combat that channel the dark side: Offense, Body, and Mind. Study all three, learn which to apply during the fury of the fight, and pass on what you have learned to your apprentice. None of this is to be kept for your own benefit. Remember, the Sith Order is more important than one Sith Lord.

**Offense** encompasses the Force skills with immediate, dynamic applications for lightsaber combat. All require relatively little exertion, so they can be easily applied at any moment. Think of Offense as a dagger saved in reserve for a fatal thrust. The skills of Offense include:

**Push:** A kinetic wave that emerges from your hands or head and can knock a single enemy off balance or scatter a group in all directions.

**Choke:** A telekinetic grip, which when centered on an enemy's neck can pinch off airflow and snap vertebrae. This requires more concentration than the Push, as well as a free hand to form the control fist. The neck is an easy target because of its soft vulnerability, but strong users of the Choke can crush an entire body, including armor.

*A strong defensive technique, and not necessarily one of the dark side. Knocking down opponents is always better than injuring them. —LUKE*

*A true master of this art can burst a walker's fuel tank, or buckle the hull of a star cruiser.*

90

CHOKE CAN EASILY LIFT ENEMIES OFF THEIR FEET.

**Inertia:** An amplification of your body's momentum that uses the Force to redirect what looks like a lumbering charge into a hooking lunge. This can surprise an enemy by making your moves unpredictable.

*No way, I'm trying this.*

*Okay, tried it. Dislocated my shoulder.*

*Vos*

**Blind:** A burst of Force energy that can overwhelm an enemy's optic nerves and render them momentarily blind.

**Throw:** A Force tactic in which you can control the path of your lightsaber when thrown. You can send it pinwheeling through clusters of ambushers before returning it to your grip. With refinement, the tactic can be used to aim and accelerate any thrown object, such as a stone or a thermal detonator.

The second school, or focus, Body, encompasses those abilities that draw from the living Force. They emanate from your own cells and affect the physical structures of others. For this reason, any cyborg limb or enhancement will hinder your ability to conjure the effects of Body. This is not your failing; it is a law of the living Force. The demands of the dark side can ravage the flesh, but fortunately it is possible to balance the scales by siphoning life from another to bolster your own.

**Lightning:** A weapon that calls forth electrical bolts from your fingertips. It is an embodiment of your wrath that can strike at the heart of your enemy. The lightning crawls across the skin and sends surges of pain through internal organs. Sustained exposure will roast flesh, calcify the skeleton, and stop the heart.

**Convection:** A concentration of Force energy that can make your fists hot to the touch, even raise their temperature to a burning intensity, but will cause no lasting injury to you. Striking an enemy with these fists can raise blisters and set robes aflame.

**Cryokinesis:** A siphoning of essence that leaches the life intensity from another, leaving behind a frost-shrouded corpse. Though this tactic usually causes the heat vitality of another being to hemorrhage, it is not possible to channel that vitality for your own use.

Sith tactics do as much harm to the user as to the victim. The dark side corrupts everything it touches. It's hard to understand why people who know this choose this path anyway.

—LUKE

TARGETS NEUTRALIZED THROUGH CONVECTION, LIGHTNING, AND CRYOKINESIS

The galaxy is choked with beings. Billions die every instant. It is better to make use of this resource. At my retreat on Byss, the life force of its colonists supplied an energy pool to sustain my dark side experiments.

**Drain life:** A delicate procedure that saps the life energy of another and funnels it directly into your own essence. It is extremely difficult to employ in combat and is derived from the teachings of Zelashiel the Blasphemer in the Holocron of Darth Revan.

**Death field:** An unstoppable concentration of dark side energy projected from your physical animus in the shape of a sphere. Any living being entering the field will wither into a dry husk. It is sustained by your will, but it will try to consume you as well.

The third school, or focus, Mind, encompasses those abilities that draw from the unifying Force. These operate on a different plane than the physical—they exist in the realm of thought and memory.

The disciplines of Mind require intense concentration and are mentally taxing. Physical strength will not help you here, only psychic clarity.

**Mind shard:** A sliver of psychic pain that is hurled from your own consciousness into your enemy's brain. If your attack succeeds, the intense agony will leave your opponent vulnerable to a lightsaber lunge. It can be difficult to establish a mental lock, but your success will improve if the ability is used in conjunction with the verbal taunts of *dun möch*.

You can use a telepathic link to calm and reassure someone, too. It's in the nature of the Sith to see only the negative.

—LUKE

**Memory walk:** A link that can open your enemy's mind and make it possible for you to compel them to relive tragic or humiliating recollections and bring forth layers of shame. Used for sustained periods, memory walk can be a sophisticated method of interrogation. The technique was stolen from the Guild of Vindicators, whose denizens are zealous about uncovering the sins of others.

94

A MIND SHARD TARGETS AN ENEMY'S INSECURITIES AND DOUBTS, THEN
SHATTERS THE ENEMY'S WILL.

95

To induce Horror, you need only confront your victim with a vision of infinity.

**Hatred:** A method of focusing your inner fire so that it can be stoked with outrage, disgust, and fear until it burns with white-hot intensity. When smashed, this furnace will radiate hatred from you in palpable waves that can send another's mind into catatonia.

**Horror:** A simple mental manipulation that can raise fear in the mind of another. By amplifying this primal emotion you can trigger horror and eventually insanity. An afflicted target will be too haunted to raise any defense.

**Crucitorn:** A technique that makes it possible to detach one's mind from coarse sensations. The secret to overcoming physical pain lies in the nonphysical. A master of this technique can endure any torture and withstand any injury.

# WILD POWER

## BY MOTHER TALZIN

# THE WRITINGS OF THE NIGHTSISTERS

My sisters, the galaxy has taken note of us, and the powerful will pay for our service. Our skills are superior, honed on the wild beasts of Dathomir.

The most skilled among our members will leave this world to act as the bodyguards and hunters of those who require the service. This will bring prosperity to your fellow sisters and honor to you.

But during your time away, you must not forget what Dathomir has given you. Although space is cold and empty, Dathomir's wilderness is lush and rich. It may be years before you return, so never forget the place that birthed and nurtured you—you will always be a Nightsister.

Among the galaxy's many species you will encounter numerous beliefs, nearly all of them claiming to be the one true belief. Not all of these contradictory ways can be true; it follows therefore that NONE are true. That realization reaffirms the wild magicks of the Daughters of Allya. Our shamanism saturates the galaxy, influencing other traditions even if their practitioners are unaware of it. It flows from a single wellspring—the life web of Dathomir.

I have served as both the shaman and the clan mother of our Nightsister tribe for many years. Most of you have never known another in this role. Through my hands and eyes, the spirits have maintained their hold on our realm. It is a core truth of the Nightsisters that the spirit plane exists parallel to our own. It is inhabited by the essences of animals, nature's forces, and our own ancestors. Yet it is ruled by the manifestations of female and male energy.

The spirits bestow fertility upon our tribe and visit us when sickness and death come upon one of our sisters as well as to claim the spirits of those who have fallen. Only here on Dathomir, however, are the two realms close enough for us to see their

shapes, and only here is there an intermediary to act on the tribe's behalf. A shaman of the Nightsisters can cross the valleys of death and dream to carry messages between the spiritual and the physical worlds.

A SHAMAN POSSESSES SIGHT THAT PERCEIVES TWO WORLDS AT ONCE.

My Master, Ky Narec, did not believe in the spirits, nor did Count Dooku or the people of Rattatak. In my eagerness to become something other than what I am, I fear I have forgotten the truth of my childhood.

Ventress

The spirits first called upon me as I lay cold and trembling, struck with a fatal affliction while birthing my first daughter. It was at that moment, suspended between life and death and bathed in the light of Dathomir's four moons, that I saw clearly the matching landscapes of both realms. It was then that I grasped how living beings are but fleshy physical shadows of their spirits and that spirits live on after their flesh has been cast aside.

THE SPIRITS BESTOW THEIR BLESSINGS.

I passed the challenge. The spirits restored my health, and I willingly became their conduit. The spirits pull upon the folds of my robe as I walk and echo beneath my voice when I speak. These writings are not merely my words but the commands of the spirits. Challenge my authority and you challenge life itself!

I SPENT A LOT OF TIME AMONG THE WITCHES OF DATHOMIR, BUT I HAVE NEVER GATHERED THIS MUCH INSIGHT INTO THE RELIGION OF THE NIGHTSISTERS. THEY MAY SELL THEIR TALENTS TO THE HIGHEST BIDDER, BUT IT DOESN'T MAKE THEM ANY LESS DEVOTED TO THEIR SPIRIT-BASED DOCTRINE. —LUKE

# THE LIVING FORCE
## AND THE DARK SIDE

Other groups, like those of the Jedi and the Sith, use strange cold terms to describe the work of the spirits. They talk of the unifying Force and the living Force— of the light side and the dark side. We must forgive their ignorance, for they are not Shamans of Dathomir. Their leaders cannot understand such concepts without enduring a trial such as mine.

There is no need to separate what they call the living Force from the unifying Force. Both are manifestations of the Twin Deities, and both are vibrantly, overwhelmingly alive. This classification of light side and dark side is also misguided. Is it evil to kill? Would those who answer yes be satisfied if predators starved so grazers could strip the land unopposed only to die amid famine? Is this the bloodless utopia envisioned by the moralistic Jedi?

What the Jedi call the dark side, Nightsisters know to be the essence of life. Even some of our witch clans have made the same error as the Jedi, ignoring those spirits' voices that call for blood and labeling them as evil. <u>My sisters, do not concern yourselves with dark side or light side. That is the language of the outsiders!</u>

Our abilities were bestowed by the spirits. The Winged Goddess and the Fanged God bestow the passive and aggressive energies that animate every creature and allow each to draw breath. Would you choose to deny yourself? Do not limit your scope by obeying artificial rules.

*This comparison is false. There IS death in nature, but there is balance, too. The mistake of the dark side is that it leads to a selfish hoarding of power. This imbalance causes harm to millions. —LUKE*

*The Nightsisters never achieved galactic power because they did not commit themselves to a single path. By refusing to name the dark side, they could not give themselves to it utterly and could never gain true power.*

# THE HISTORY OF DATHOMIR

How do we know our homeworld is unique among all the planets of the cosmos? I have a shaman's eyes, and I have seen the proof. I have watched the spirits travel from one realm to another by means of a smoky tether that is anchored in our forests. If you study the histories of the outsiders, you will find only validation of my words. Throughout recorded time, great civilizations have always been drawn to Dathomir.

The packs of rhoa kwi, which hunt in the scrub fringe of the tar pits, are the primitive descendants of intelligent beings called the Kwa. They once held the favor of the spirits. The Kwa built Infinity Gates to travel to other stars, but their machines created unnatural voids and wounded Dathomir. Angry, the spirits summoned the Rakata Empire to demolish the Kwa. The spirits forced the Kwa back to their animal state so they might never again work technology.

RUINS OF THE INFINITY GATE AT THE AERIE OF KOROTAS

The Infinity Gates are dormant but still operational. One coven of Nightsisters tried to activate them before the Clone Wars. My Empire must seize this technology and map the extent of the Kwa teleportation network.

Over the millennia, the spirits called many other groups to Dathomir for purposes of their own. The Paecians came, made their homes here, and had many children. So, too, did the Sith. They recognized the raw power of Dathomir but could not perceive its true shape.

Many years after the Sith abandoned their Dathomir academies, the Jedi exiled one of their own to this world. You know her as Allya, mother of all witches. Allya held the favor of the spirits, and her daughters became the first crafters of spirit-willed magicks.

MOTHER ALLYA'S ARRIVAL ON DATHOMIR

Centuries later, the Jedi returned. Their great training ship, the Chu'unthor, was called to our shores, and the Jedi who came to reclaim it could not match our strength. Even their Master Yoda, the strongest of all the Jedi, abandoned the prize and fled.

Few visitors have come to Dathomir since then. But the Nightsisters spread throughout the galaxy after I unified the clans following the defeat of Mother Zalem. By performing missions and services for others, we are making the galaxy aware of our ways and enforcing the will of the spirits.

*And as a child I was given over to the criminal Hal'sted. Was this the will of the spirits, Mother? I have often had my doubts.*

*Ventress*

*I heard the story a little differently. Yoda negotiated a truce with Mother Rell and left the shipwreck in peace. And Mother Rell was definitely not a Nightsister. —Luke*

# THE HISTORY OF THE NIGHTSISTERS

It is a blessing to be born on Dathomir . . . and a burden. We are the favored people of the spirits and much is expected of us. We must not mar our home with the pollution of technology. We must obey our clan mothers and shamans. We must revere the rituals that bind the physical and spiritual realms. With such simple edicts, it is disappointing that so many witches have failed to obey them.

The writings of Allya teach that those who choose ignorance will never know greatness, and those who fear death will never achieve power. But after Allya's death, some of her daughters—perhaps weakened by the Jedi blood in their veins—added to Allya's words by introducing "good" and "evil." They claimed Allya had espoused this blasphemy during the last moments of her life. These witches called this altered text the Book of Law.

Those who rejected this altered text and held true to Allya's pure words became the first Nightsisters. Our Nightsister ancestors were banished from the home clans for their beliefs. But among their fellow believers, they restored the text to Allya's original teachings—to the balance of the physical realm and the spirit realm. They named their volume the Book of Shadows. In the past, competing Nightsister clans have coexisted, each led by a clan mother and a shaman—except in cases where the two figures are one and the same. But I have united my warring sisters into a single coven.

*I plan to construct an Imperial orbital base above Dathomir and a prison upon its surface. It will be curious to see what the Nightsisters do. I will contain them if they seek to escape their cage.*

THE SPIRITS SPEAK THROUGH THE CLAN MOTHER, REVEALING THE
WISDOM OF THE BOOK OF SHADOWS.

Every witch of Dathomir knows that males lack the ability the females possess to balance the twin calls of the Winged Goddess and Fanged God. Males are simpler, more beastlike. We honor our Nightbrothers, but among our clan we recognize that they serve the spirits better when kept in isolation. In the past, other clans integrated their males as servants or slaves, but our Nightbrothers are kept separated until summoned. In their compound, they naturally form a packlike structure and channel their virile energy into combat training.

*The Nightbrothers are adequate fighters but are ill-served in isolation. They could learn much more under the direct tutelage of a Nightsister.*

*Ventress*

# THE WINGED GODDESS

In the spirit realm, the Winged Goddess appears as a blinding-white gryphon. It is she who governs fertility and growth, and she who acts as a mediator to reconcile wounded parties. She knows everything that has occurred and everything that is yet to come.

Channeling the Winged Goddess brings forth great quantities of spirit ichor into the physical realm. This ichor appears as green smoke, but it can be given physical shape and mass as well as be manipulated in spellcasting by a gifted shaman such as myself.

A skilled shaman <u>may conjure objects from raw spirit ichor</u>. The conjured object is everlasting and can take many forms such as a hunting lance or a goblet of boiled blackroot. Divination and scrying are achieved by shaping the spirit ichor into a sphere and peering into its depths. Through scrying, a shaman can view events occurring anywhere in the galaxy. Divination or heartshadow, calls forth visions of possible futures. Through this art, I have learned the fall of empires yet to come and how to protect the Nightsisters from those who would seek to exploit us.

In spellcasting, spirit ichor can become the waters of life and be used to heal wounds or restore memories. When used in conjunction with crafters chanting incantations, I can channel the ichor to rejuvenate the near-dead by coaxing the injured spirit to emerge from hibernation.

Mesmerism is another gift provided by spirit ichor. This power allows a shaman to override the thoughts of those weaker than oneself—particularly men and

Only a shaman like Mother Talzin can create objects from spirit. I have tried and failed. Those who can use this art can never be disarmed. —Ventress

SEEING INTO THE FUTURE IS AN ASPECT OF THE UNIFYING FORCE, BUT YODA WARNED ME THAT THE FUTURE IS ALWAYS CHANGING. WE HAVE THE POWER TO MAKE OUR OWN DESTINIES.

—LUKE

A PURE STRAND OF SPIRIT ICHOR, PULLED DIRECTLY FROM THE OTHER REALM

offworlders. A tap of the fingertip to the victim's forehead will induce a trancelike state and make the victim powerless to refuse your commands.

Another form of control is achieved by crafting a small statue of a victim, combining a strand of hair and a roiling cauldron brimming with the waters of life. This crude figure may then be stabbed with wooden needles or weakened with a breath of miasma. Any harm done to the totem will be felt by the victim it resembles. But nothing comes without a cost. The effort required of the shaman to summon such quantities of ichor can prove exhausting.

I do not wish to disturb the Winged Goddess with endless supplications, but in times of severe distress, I have used the shaman's connection to directly invoke the spirits. When the call succeeds, the specters of long-ago warriors will glow into view. Heralded by a rush of wind, they will charge a target while uttering a shriek that emanates from every direction at once.

# THE FANGED GOD

The Fanged God appears as a night-black gargoyle in the spirit realm. He governs virility and the hunt. He also communicates smells, sounds, and tastes. He is the counterpart to the Winged Goddess and is equally important to the governance of the spirit realm. As Nightsisters, you draw from both pools and thus keep the universal energies in balance.

The magic of the Fanged God is so powerful that channeling it can burst minor blood vessels in our physical bodies, raising telltale bruises on the cheeks and around the eyes. These marks were once considered scars of shame by the passive witches who revered the Book of Law. Yet they are brands of honor. Our tradition of facial tattooing reclaims this history for ourselves and announces to the galaxy that we are Nightsisters. And while our Nightbrothers are kept separated, they are marked as our kin and our warriors by the tattooing on their chests and faces.

CLAN ALLEGIANCES AND WARRIOR TRIUMPHS ARE WRITTEN ON THE SKIN.

It is the Fanged God who conjures up the Wild Hunt each year, when the moons are at their brightest and the snows have vanished from the slopes of the Shattered Ridge. I have seen the dark figures with glowing pale eyes as they gallop through the forest. I have heard their hunt-calls as they carry those who cross in their path back to the abode of the ethereal riders.

The Fanged God is close to you at all times. He seeps through the border separating the two realms and does not require as much effort to channel. Every time you fight or feast or bleed, you are communing with the Fanged God.

As girls you learned to speak with our planet's native rancors and to ride them. The realm beyond shadows contains a single ur-spirit for each of the galaxy's animal species. And just as you did with rancors, so can you do with the ur-spirits. Once you acquire the tongue of a particular ur-spirit, you can understand any creature of that type. Once you can communicate with the creature, you can calm it. Once you can calm it, you can control it. The most skilled Nightsisters who study this art hold the rank of beastwarden.

A MOUNTED RANCOR EQUIPPED FOR A RIVER CROSSING

THESE ABILITIES ALL COME FROM THE LIVING FORCE. IT'S A SOURCE OF POSITIVE ENERGY, BUT LIKE ANYTHING, IT CAN BE TAKEN TO EXTREMES. LOSING YOURSELF TO YOUR ANIMAL NATURE LEADS YOU TO THE DARK SIDE. WITHOUT CONTROL, IT'S FAR TOO EASY TO BECOME SAVAGE. —LUKE

Because the Fanged God governs the hunt, he is present during tracking, sacrifice, and the drinking of blood. He can sharpen your perceptions to set you on the path of the most elusive prey even when you are far from Dathomir. It is he who gifts us with the _blood trail_, a technique in which you place a drop of your own blood on your target and use that link to track your quarry across the stars. It is a technique known only to the Nightsisters.

_The blood trail is how I hunted the Warlords of Rattatak, even after they had surrendered their thrones and hid from me in strongholds of exile._

_Ventress_

*These are not so different from Sith amulets, despite what the Dathomiri preach. Yet none of these abilities have yet been duplicated by a Sith alchemist, to my knowledge. Curious.*

# TALISMANS AND TOTEMS

As clan shaman, it is within my power to entreat the spirits. Because the Nightsisters are their favored children, they may agree to empower a receptacle in the physical realm where their essence will sleep until summoned. These receptacles, crafted by shamans into talismans and totems, may hold their power for generations.

Talismans are often gems set in rings or pendants. Totems are carved objects depicting an animal or a spirit entity. When kept within a dwelling, these objects offer a blessing to all who pass through the doorway. Those who swallow a totem will release all its energy into themselves—though their omnipotence will last only moments. For when the spirit is released from the object, it returns to the spirit realm and reduces the body to ash.

Talismans of Transformation allow the wearer to change shape in the physical realm, to become an animal and tap into the animal's spirit essence, for example. The Nightsisters possess several Talismans of Transformation—the bolma, the brackaset, the eollu, and the burra fish. One of our sisters has yet to return the Talisman of the Raven. The Talisman of Age taps into the animal nature of humans, and briefly restores the vigor of youth.

A TALISMAN OF TRANSFORMATION WORKS ITS CHANGE.

Talismans of Finding are shaped to resemble a compass and will guide the user to any target that has been imprinted upon it. Talismans of Resurrection can bring the spirits of the dead back to their physical bodies. It is vital to remember, however, that if much time has passed, their forms may be little more than fetid skeletons. Finally, Talismans of Counterspell offer protection from the magicks of others by deflecting curses back onto their casters.

Totems of the Elementals can summon Night, Sunlight, Smoke, Ice, Flame, Clay, and Woodrot. These are powerful, primal entities, so they may not always obey your bidding. Totems of Familiars are more welcoming. They will call an animal to your side and hold the animal there as long as you possess the totem. The summoned beast is blessed with magick. The energies of these familiars help crafters accomplish some of the most difficult magicks.

Had I possessed this as a child, I could have saved the life of my Master. I see that Mother Talzin guards her treasures jealously. *Ventress*

# BEASTS OF DATHOMIR

The living creatures of our home are too numerous to name. They create a life web that is stronger than those found on any other planet in the galaxy. This is because Dathomir is a conduit to the spirit realm, and the keystone upon which all reality is balanced.

Skilled Nightsisters can channel the abilities of Dathomiri beasts they have never met simply by recognizing their spirit scents. While you're in other parts of the galaxy, it is essential to your success that you frequently reacquaint yourself with our brother and sister animals. When you know their natures, you can better channel their qualities. The practice will also reestablish your connection with the life web if you have spent too many days among the machines of the offworlders—especially the accursed mausoleum of glass and steel called Coruscant.

The great rancor is the ruler of all beasts on Dathomir. Spawned from the ferocity of the Fanged God and the insight of the Winged Goddess, it is a fierce fighter that rakes with its claws and tears with its powerful teeth. Yet rancors are wise and tender toward their own. Their arms help them swing through the canopy to hunt screeching purboles, and their massive legs propel their lumbering runs when they pursue fleeing bolma herds. The Nightsisters connect with them, speak to them, and ride them. Be like the rancor, and you will hold authority in any confrontation you face among outsiders.

THE KEEPERS FORCED JABBA'S RANCOR INTO A DUNGEON WHERE IT COULD BARELY MOVE. IT WAS HALF-STARVED. THOUGH I DIDN'T HAVE A CHOICE, I'M STILL SORRY I HAD TO KILL IT. —LUKE

ONE OF THE MIGHTY RANCORS OF THE DREAMING RIVER

The drebbin and the ssurrians are also major predators on Dathomir. Their thick hides allow them to ignore most irritants, and other creatures have learned to back away when they see one of these creatures for fear they will disappear in a snap of teeth. Like the drebbin and the ssurrians, we do not need to change or accommodate those smaller and weaker than us.

Other beasts of the wild that do not have the biggest muscles or the sharpest claws possess more devious methods to achieve their ends. The artery worm strikes from inside, traveling the blood upstream and killing its host in exquisite agony when it reaches the heart. The voritor lizard and the Kodashi viper trade size for poison, and announce their malevolence with bright colors and vivid patterns. Remember this when donning the clothing, markings, and weapons of a Nightsister. An intimidating appearance will frighten away those who are not fully committed to a fight.

A SISTER OF THE VORITOR GUARDS THE BORDERS OF NIGHTSISTER LANDS.

Every time we eat the meat of a whuffa worm or wear its skin, we are reminded that life is connected. Look at the qibbit bird, which picks the scraps from the rancor's teeth. The rancor is cleaned, the bird is fed, and both parties benefit.

Like the wild animals, regardless of size, you are never defenseless. Small threats can be deadly threats. Consider the sparkfly, which has a sting that contains all the energy of the sky's lightning. Or the scissorfist, which has claws that when latched on to an attacker's skin can never be pried apart. Even the mighty rancor may be felled by shear mites, which can chew through its hide with their acid-laced mandibles. Do not fear your enemies. Life always persists—even a savage, blood-drenched death only returns your spirit to the realm beyond shadows.

It has been difficult, commanding droids. They move like living things yet have no presence in the Force and no spirit sense.

Ventress

It is for precisely this reason that artificial beings are well suited for combat against Jedi. What better way to guarantee a drawn-out war?

This is not an excuse. To kill another intelligent being is to override his or her will, and it should only be done when there's no other choice. The fate of a spirit should have no bearing on our decisions in the here and now.

—Luke

# Nature's Vigor

The echoes of the Fanged God can be heard throughout the air of Dathomir, from the sound of the snuffling moogs hidden in their lairs to the screeches of the archixes circling their aeries atop the Singing Mountain. The ur-spirits of animals are red and raw, but the twin spirit of plants pulses with a deep green.

You are an animal yourself and still a part of Dathomir's life web, even when you find yourself inside a hollow metal starship around a cold star. You can always tap into the power of the spirits. Fan the fires of your bestial nature, and you will share the abilities of the beasts themselves.

Predators possess a degree of awareness that we do not. By invoking the ability known as the Sense of the Veshet, you will distinguish scents carried on the wind from hundreds of meters away and will be able to see into blackness even when the moons have hid their faces. If you invoke the Ears of the Chiroptix, you will hear whispers and be able to paint pictures of hidden places from their sounds.

Some beasts must be nimble to avoid predators as well as to catch their prey. By invoking the Speed of the Toocha, you will be imbued with short bursts of blindingly fast speed and energized leaps to cover remarkable distance. Both can be useful for escape or surprise. Invoking the Touch of the Kiin'Dray applies a binding force to your hands and feet, enabling you to scramble up a cliff face or to hold a weapon in a grip no one can break.

The whuffa's power of regeneration has a host of combat uses. The Revitalization of the Whuffa can refresh the body or, if one's will is sufficient, allow the regrowth of a limb. The Scream of the Ssurrian can bring forth the deep, thrumming vibrations of the great dragon's hunting call, as well as the earsplitting shriek of its territorial warning. When directed at an enemy, the wave of sound will pop eardrums and shatter teeth.

THE TOUCH OF THE KIIN'DRAY

### Surge of the Brier

Compared to the animal essences, the green spirits of the plants are quieter and more content, but they are not without uses. Invoking them will generate the calming aura of meditation or break down a poison once it has infected the bloodstream. With Surge of the Brier, you can reach into the spirit realm and grip the essence of a sessile plant. Pull and twist the plant's physical form into a shape of your choosing. By doing this you can wrap enemies in vines or impale them with thorns.

Even weather has a spirit. Its formless expanse glows with the blue-black hue of the heavens before moonsrise. The Aspect of the Storm will allow you to shape this inky fabric into the bright white threads of lightning strikes.

Deeper summoning will bring forth winds that can carry you through the sky. The air may also carry you aloft within a green sphere of energy, just as foam rises from a churning waterfall. Within this bubble you are protected from enemies while hurling lightning on their heads.

# Training a Warrior

The means to produce the finest warriors and assassins in the galaxy are at our fingertips, and they have commanded the highest prices on the galactic market. Our abilities are paying off. If you have left our fold, know that your service sustains us and validates our traditions.

You are an agent of the Nightsisters, and more must follow in your path. If you do not have a current assignment, you should train others to achieve your rank. All Nightsisters and Nightbrothers have trained since they were young to use our weapons: the pike, the mace, the spear, the ax, and the chain-sickle. Those worthy to become warriors or assassins must be tested to prove their skill. In the arena of the Crucible, the candidates face three tests—the tests of Fury, Night, and Elevation. Any who fails a test will be eliminated. When the prize is to be the servant of a Sith Lord, elimination equals death.

Ventress

In the Test of Fury, the candidates are pitted against one another or against their instructor. Some may form alliances for advantage, whereas others may stand alone against all challengers. Either response is useful in determining a candidate's temperament for battle.

No quarter is given during the Test of Fury.

THE SLOW AND THE CLUMSY WILL NOT PASS THE TEST OF ELEVATION.

When the moons are low and all light has been extinguished, the Test of Night may be held. The candidates fight much like they do in the Test of Fury, but without eyesight. Some candidates may exhibit preternatural senses or a gift for stealth. Some may even have the presence of mind to channel Ears of the Chiroptix.

During the Test of Elevation, the Crucible's moving pillars are activated. Combatants are left unsure of their footing, as if fighting on shifting sand. Those with cunning will use the stone blocks as cover for ambushes. Those with aggression will use the high ground to pounce upon their prey. The most skilled candidates will not only survive the Crucible, but will dominate the battles. These are the most fit for a future offworld assignment.

*The Nightsisters are ruthless in their training.*
*I collected the most skilled Zabrak Nightbrothers*
*before blockading Dathomir.*

# Instruction and Transformation

Those who pass the tests of the Crucible may be suited for further training. There are three categories of skill we offer offworld clients: hunter, warrior, and shadow killer. But no matter what your role, you should always wear the clothing and accoutrements that brand you as Dathomiri, for through your visibility our reputation will spread.

Hunters should wear the red hoods and robes like the blood trail they follow, as well as black wrist wraps to protect from the sting of their weapon. A hunter wields an energy bow with a plasma bowstring and arrows of the same material. The energy bow can fire plasma arrows unerringly at any target, and its bowstring can blind or burn should you need to use it as a bludgeon. It is a specialty weapon. Therefore, it is vital that our clan be supplied with the standard nine credits from every ten you earn, so we may continue to outfit you with the equipment you require.

*I HAVE SPENT A LOT OF TIME ON DATHOMIRI BUT THESE WEAPONS ARE EXOTIC AND EXTREMELY RARE.*

*—LUKE*

A HUNTER'S SKILL WITH THE ENERGY BOW INFLUENCES THE REPUTATION OF ALL NIGHTSISTERS FOR GOOD OR ILL.

Shadow killers are assassins. They wear black wraps of the night and carry silent weapons, such as the dagger and the poison dart. It is an art to become one with the dark. Shadow killers can also be aided by spirit ichor. Shamans, such as I, can conjure a mist that allows our shadow killers to operate midway between the physical realm and the spirit realm.

Our warriors wear the cuffs and shoulder armor of those who have withstood the Crucible. Their weapons, such as pikes, are infused with powerful magick and can cut through any substance.

A SKILLED SHADOW KILLER CAN VANISH FROM SIGHT.

I have also empowered lesser minions with the dark side.

Through the magicks of the Fanged God, a warrior can be transformed into an avatar of primal anger. This requires the skill of an expert shaman and a full coven of crafters. By conjuring green spirit ichor and channeling the rawest hatred, the energies can be siphoned into hulking muscle and bone. A transformed warrior will be massive, standing a head taller, boasting a broad chest and spine-crushing arms. A proud Zabrak of the Nightbrothers will grow a crown of horns to rival that of a verne buck in autumn.

A WARRIOR'S TRUE STRENGTH LIES NOT IN MUSCLE BUT IN ANGER.

Although the Crucible tests a candidate's skill, it is not the end of their training. It is a second beginning. Candidates who reach this point are skilled in combat, but they lack the subtle touch needed to channel the abilities of the spirits. Emotion is a powerful catalyst that connects you to your bestial essence and, by extension, to the ur-spirits that rule our natural impulses. To strengthen these abilities, order candidates to accomplish a task that requires utter concentration—then distract them with mocking taunts and the agony of a barbed lash. There is no shorter path to the revelation that it is not peace but passion that leads to achievement.

Train your students well. It has been foretold by Allya that a perfect being will one day arise—one brought into existence by the spirits and one who will embody the balance between the Winged Goddess and the Fanged God. Perhaps it will be you who will train this champion. Perhaps it is you.

*Many cultures have an obsession with prophecy and the rise of a future savior. If you wait for others to rule, you will never become a ruler.*

THOSE WHO FOLLOW THE DARK SIDE ALWAYS MISTAKE THEIR POWER AS PROOF THAT THEY HAVE FOUND THE WAY. YES, THE DARK SIDE OFFERS POWER, BUT IT'S POWER WITHOUT CONTROL OR DIRECTION. THOSE WHO WIELD IT LACK THE ABILITY TO DO SO WISELY.

—LUKE

# COMPETING DARK SIDE TRADITIONS

We reject the term "dark side," but it is commonly applied because of the cultural pull of the Jedi and the Sith. Those who use the powers of the supernatural—or, as others call it, the Force—in order to kill at their employer's behest are considered dark siders. It is clear that if we are to be thus classified, we should market ourselves as such.

You will find yourself among many who do not understand our traditions. They may call you Sith, or any number of other prominent traditions. Use this chance to set the Nightsisters apart in the minds of those who hold power. Only by promoting our unique skills will we be able to continue to command a premium price.

The Prophets of the Dark Side are similar to the Sith in many ways. Their breakaway religion splintered from the teachings of a Sith Lord, Darth Millennial, but the Prophets are not warriors. They claim to possess unparalleled skill in fortune-telling, and some have approached our clients promising to reveal the outcomes of galactic events yet to come. I doubt the spirits whisper to them with any clarity, and only a witch in the grip of insanity would be charmed by their religion. I suspect their pronouncements are empty shells made from self-fulfilling statements. Plant this seed of doubt if the opportunity arises.

I have met these reclusive chetins and listened to their singsong prophecies. They do possess the gift of futuresight, which proved useful to my forces at the Battle of Dromund Kaas. But the Prophets themselves admit they have hunted down heretics and imitators. _Ventress_

PROPHET OF THE DARK SIDE

New claimants to the dark side tradition have arisen from the farthest reaches of the galaxy. The Kanzer Exiles are a group of reptilians from the Valtaullu Rift who claim allegiance to their Lord Ravager. And the Knell of Muspilli is a death cult that dwells amid the moon-trees of the Gunninga Gap. Whether these groups are true representatives or merely opportunists is unclear. However, their claims to power are quite specific. The Kanzer Exiles assert that they have the power to enslave many minds at once. The Knell alleges to have the abilities to summon apocalyptic deities from the realm beyond shadows. If either group should fail to fulfill these declarations, we will have our evidence to expose its memebers as frauds.

The most enigmatic of the new competitors are the Sorcerers of Rhand. They claim a kinship with the dark, which they view as the embodiment of decay and death. A true Sorcerer is said to be able to use a psychic blast to eradicate an object or a living being. They are not believed to operate outside the Nihil Retreat, but make an effort to learn more of their ways if you can.

ONE OF THE ROTTING SORCERERS OF RHAND

LORD SHADOWSPAWN STUDIED UNDER THE SORCERERS OF RHAND. HE COULD HAVE COLLAPSED THE FRAGILE NEW REPUBLIC IF I HADN'T BEEN FORCED TO CONFRONT HIM AT MINDOR.
—LUKE

*This isn't nearly as impressive a feat as the witch believed. The Mecrosa Order survived the Cleansing of the Nine Houses, but all its Sith and Force-sensitive members were wiped out.*

Other groups have been in this game of dark side mercenaries for centuries, far longer than the Nightsisters. These are our prime competitors. Do what you must to dissolve their hold among the powerful of the Core and Rim.

The influence of the Tapani sector's royal houses is strong. Among House Mecetti's nobles there are those who claim affinity with the Sith, and whose ancestors triggered the Cleansing of the Nine Houses, which not only destabilized an entire quadrant of the galaxy but swallowed three other noble houses. The agents of House Mecetti belong to the Mecrosa Order. They specialize in assassination. I know our skills are superior, for I sent three shadow killers to the Pella system to test their skills. Two of ours returned, but <u>none of the Mecrosa opponents survived.</u>

*Count Dooku has close ties with House Mecetti. I hope he has heard of this.*
*Ventress*

A MEMBER OF THE MECROSA ORDER

*I have my own agents among the Blackguard.*
*Any secrets they uncover become mine soon after.*

The Blackguard operates from the molten world of Mustafar. They are largely recluses and have sought dark side lore since they emerged from the ruins of Sith philosophy after the Battle of Ruusan nearly a thousand years ago. The Blackguard clings to the principle that acquiring knowledge is superior to exerting physical power. It makes them a careful and cautious rival. For now, they are too isolated to factor into our plans.

THE BLACKGUARD ARE NOT YET A THREAT TO THE NIGHTSISTERS.

The Shapers of Kro Var are few in number, but they profess to be shamans of a similar tradition to our own. I do not doubt they have gained a small glimpse into the spirit realm, but they are not native to Dathomir. They cannot have heard the call of the spirits as clearly as we have. The Shapers of Kro Var use dark magick to manipulate the elements of air, earth, water, and fire. They have recently made their services available to buyers in the Marzoon sector.

MISGUIDED THEY MAY BE, BUT THE SHAPERS OF KRO VAR GAIN THEIR POWERS FROM THE SPIRITS.

Only the clan mothers may broker the services of the Nightsisters. But not all Nightsisters have equal expertise. We will not repeat the mistakes of Shaman Yansu Grjak, who too eagerly sold the services of her clan to Separatist buyers and then could not protect her sisters from the Jedi counterattack.

By offering your services, you agree to perform any mission on your client's behalf, provided it falls under the terms brokered by the clan mother. The Nightsisters will not tolerate dishonor, no matter who provides the funding. Those who treat us as if we were primitives to be swindled will be punished—a warning to others and further evidence of our lethal aptitude.

*At times, Mother Talzin shows more concern for reputation than the will of the spirits.*

*Ventress*

THE JEDI ARE NOT, NOR HAVE THEY EVER BEEN, MERCENARIES. THE FORCE IS A GIFT TO BE USED TO PROTECT ALL BEINGS, ESPECIALLY THE POWERLESS. SELLING FORCE-POWERED SERVICES FOR CREDITS IS SELFISH AND HARMS THOSE WHO NEED HELP THE MOST.

—LUKE

# The Science of Creating Life

What is the Force? The Jedi say it is created by life. But I say the Force creates life. It is a simple deduction—an obvious conclusion when supported by structured experimentation. Yet consider this: the galaxy's leading scientific minds are largely ignorant of the Force, and the galaxy's most skilled Force-users reject science. The latter are caught up in romantic mysticism, convinced they have been called by a higher power. The former have no excuse.

Thus, I will be the first to pursue this line of inquiry. A scientific understanding of the Force is not the same as the memorization of incantations. Science seeks to understand the principle behind a reaction, not merely how to replicate it—particularly when the formulas for the reactions are bloated with centuries of empty ornamentation.

To study alchemy, one must strip away its rhyming phrases and its perverse obsession with blood sacrifice. To study a shamanistic talisman, one must look beyond the words of invocation. When a talisman unleashes its power, what is the true trigger? The words? The speaker's tone? His mental state? If a talisman's power resides inside the gem, what will happen if a fragment is shaved off, then another? Does the energy dissipate when sufficient mass is lost? Is the ratio consistent for similar gems and similar talismans?

The Sith of old never asked these questions, for tradition and obedience extinguished their spark of curiosity. And these questions are much more than idle speculation. My science will remove everything superfluous. In this way, the true nature of the fundamental elements that the Jedi and the Sith wield so casually will be revealed.

THE ELEMENT THAT PLAGUEIS COULDN'T MEASURE IS THE WILL OF THE FORCE.
THE JEDI HEAR THIS CALL, AND I BELIEVE THE SITH DO, TOO.
I DON'T THINK THE FORCE FELT COMPELLED TO SPEAK TO PLAGUEIS.
—LUKE

So it must be that I am the first. I will change it all. The Sith wallowed in ritual even during our centuries under the Rule of Two, playing dress-up in frightening costumes and posturing for our followers. I will burn away the colorful wrappings and study the skeletal structure that reveals the architecture of reality.

My ultimate goal is the secret of life—that life that gives us consciousness, for without consciousness each of us is nothing. Through science, I will create new life and sustain my own. There is no reason why Darth Plagueis could not live forever.

> I do not share my former Master's enthusiasm for process. I care only for results.

# Influencing the Midi-Chlorians

The Force is found throughout the universe, not only in living things. Everything in existence that draws upon various aspects of the energy we call the Force may be classified into three categories.

The aperion includes and unites all matter, giving it shape and cohesion. Aspects of the aperion include gravity and electromagnetism—though the term encompasses everything in both space and time. Many of the abilities understood as belonging to the Unifying Force are tied to the aperion.

The anima gives life—but not thought—to animals, plants, and other living beings. Midi-chlorians are responsible for inducing and sustaining anima in almost all species. Many of the living Force abilities are tied to the anima.

The pneuma is the expression of conscious thought. Thinking, self-aware minds contribute to the collective pneuma, which is accessed by many naturally telepathic species, as well as by the various mind tricks of the Jedi and the Sith.

hese fundamental forces would exist even without midi-chlorians. However, midi-chlorians are the beneficiaries of an unusually strong connection to all forms of physical and psychic energy. Because the midi-chlorians inhabit living cells, the host organism is able to draw upon this connection. Midi-chlorians are endosymbionts. They die when their host dies, and o host can live if completely purged of midi-chlorians.

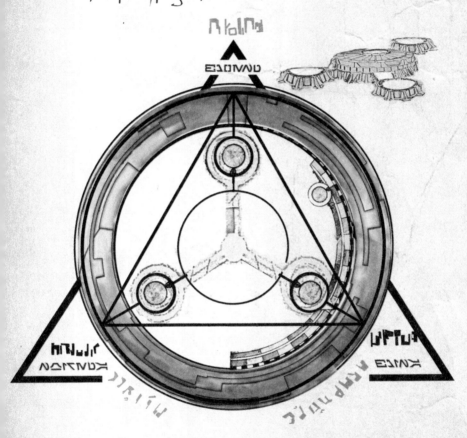

The visible biology of the cell and its midi-chlorians is a product of the invisible interactions of the aperion, anima, and pneuma.

THE ENTIRE FOCUS ON MIDI-CHLORIANS IS MISGUIDED. THEY ARE A NATURAL LESSON IN SYMBIOSIS. WHEN WE LISTEN TO THE SMALLEST CREATURES, THEY OPEN US TO THE EXPANSE OF THE FORCE. ONLY A SITH WOULD SEEK TO DISMANTLE A RELATIONSHIP THAT BENEFITS BOTH PARTIES.

—LUKE

All living things, regardless of their planet of origin, appear to possess midi-chlorians or complementary biological structures. The reasons for this isomorphism are unknown. But the results of my experiments into abiogenesis have shifted my present focus significantly. Of considerable interest is the fact that, while most cellular organelles generate chemical energy, midi-chlorians generate Force energy. They also appear to possess a single unified consciousness linked via the pneuma and can be influenced by the host's mental state. In particular, negative emotions such as the loss of hope can induce cellular necrosis.

Typical blood concentration is around 2,500 midi-chlorians per cell. Cutting this concentration in half will usually induce death. I conclude that Force energy is required for life and that midi-chlorians are its biological vector.

Jedi and Sith have high midi-chlorian counts at the moments of their births. Breeding between two Force-sensitive parents is an option, as the pairings generally result in Force-sensitive offspring. On the other hand, genetic defects have been a concern since the inbreeding among the royals of Vjun during their mad chase for extraordinary powers. A simple blood transfusion is the obvious answer, but I have found that the subject's native midi-chlorians will reject the influx of foreign cells.

*The writings of my Master betray his narrow focus. In his obsession to unlock life's secrets, he proved blind to immediate threats.*

# Perpetual Life.

The solution, therefore, is not to introduce new midi-chlorians but to impose one's will on the midi-chlorians already present in the subject. This can be done through the energy of the pneuma. Just as a warrior in peak condition can lift a heavy weight, so can someone with a sharpened mental focus and an affinity for the Force achieve a measurable effect on living cells.

I began with experiments on scurriers and other small creatures. I used my will, amplified through my body's own midi-chlorians, to override the lesser concentrated midi-chlorian voices in the test subjects. This proved more challenging than I predicted. Because midi-chlorians are linked by a universal mind, the ones in my own cells seemed to resist this imposition upon their fellows. But eventually I succeeded, first with small creatures, then with slaves purchased from the Hutts. I forced the midi-chlorians to override their natural life cycles.

What I discovered is that these midi-chlorians would not die. Instead, they drew upon sustaining Force energy, which acted on a microscopic level to halt tissue decay in their host, putting an end to aging and disease.

Vaqué's was indeed the first to influence midi-chlorians to create life. I did not understand his work, but I am happy to take advantage of its results. My Shi'ido scientists have grown some fascinating mutants.

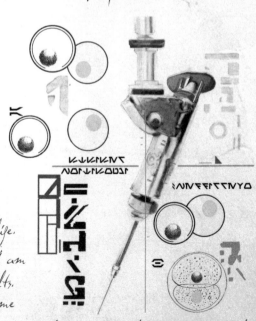

I guide the nanosyringes with microscopic nudges in the Force.

## Concentrating the Force

My experiments proved midi-chlorians could be
controlled. If this is true, then could they not also
be induced to create life at the monocellular level?
Midi-chlorians in the cells of a mother could, in
theory, be persuaded to craft a zygote.

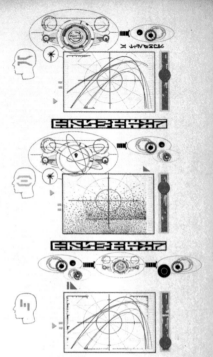

For consistency in my test subjects, I obtained
hundreds of identical humanoids, each with
a consistent midi-chlorian level. After much
experimentation, I succeeded in prodding the
midi-chlorians to replicate themselves through
asexual fission. Though in most cases, this process
increased the numbers uncontrollably and
killed the host.

Thousands of subjects were classified and discarded
during biological testing. A pity more could not have been
used, as it would have made the data more conclusive.

But I believe that by using this method I can trick midi-chlorians into creating a zygote.
Then it would simply be a matter of growing the subject under normal biological conditions.
Such a subject could, of course, take years to hit the developmental milestones of a typical
humanoid, but he could have a midi-chlorian count as high as 20,000 per cell. That is
more than any Jedi or Sith in recorded history. Although entirely theoretical, such an
achievement is intriguing.

If new life could be created where none existed before, the living could sustain their
bodies indefinitely. Science has led to these conclusions, yet these secrets must
be guarded with utmost care. For now, it remains purely theoretical.

I CAN'T HELP FEELING A CHILL AS I READ THIS ACCOUNT BY PLAGUEIS,
KNOWING THAT MY FATHER WAS KNOWN FOR HIS HIGH MIDI-CHLORIAN
COUNT, WHICH WAS SUPPOSEDLY EVEN HIGHER THAN YODA'S.

—LUKE

# The Philosophy of Life

The secrets of immortality are not meant for common beings. If all knew these truths, it would destabilize the structure of civilization. I do not wish to live in a galaxy where any fool can perpetuate his ignorance for eternity.

Life is not mystical. Like Tibanna gas or nova crystals, life is a resource to be exploited. It is unique in that those who possess it find it priceless; yet, in the aggregate, it is so common that it is functionally worthless. Billions of beings come into existence every day, and billions more die. We should preserve only those who advance our goals or whose work is complementary to our own. Under my Grand Plan, this list will include apprentices, researchers, and credit-worshipping corporate executives.

But all other beings must be allowed to die. I would not turn the controls of an airspeeder over to a gundark, and I will not leave the dull masses in charge of issues that matter. They are ultimately content with their brief lives. They would not know what to do with the gift of never-ending time.

Immortality opens up a new tactic for the Grand Plan. No longer do I need to prepare for the succession of the Sith Order after my death. Schemes in politics and finance set in motion today can safely take decades or even centuries to come to fruition. Such subtle plays are ideal for the Grand Master whose patience is infinite.

> DURING THE BATTLE OF MINDOR, I FACED THE REALITY THAT EVERYTHING IN THIS UNIVERSE EVENTUALLY PERISHES. No one wants to die. But this obsession with extending life is selfish. We all have our time. Nothing good comes from trying to cheat it.
> —LUKE

*Alas, the tale of Darth Plagueis the Wise became a tragedy. It seems that sustaining life was not the same as protecting oneself from injury. Or from accident.*

135

# New Explorations in the Force

My work with midi-chlorians is rooted in what is traditionally considered the living Force, or those energies attached to the anima and the pneuma. The unifying Force, or the aperion, is not specifically necessary for the creation and manipulation of life, but midi-chlorians channel it nonetheless. As I look at the Force in a new light, I have found new applications for these omnipresent states.

The aperion governs the cohesion of matter, from the atoms of a pebble to all planets and gravity in the universe. This includes the dimension of time. Through the aperion, space-time may be manipulated on a grand scale—that is if a user channels sufficient energy through his aggregate midi-chlorians while maintaining focus and accuracy.

I believe an individual could step instantly from one place to another by folding space, regardless of the intervening distance. Similarly, one could be able to fold time—not to temporally displace a physical object, but to shift one's consciousness backward and forward along time's flow. Such a thing would permit the study of all knowledge through history, even the secrets recorded in the long-lost Library of Silversisi.

IF THESE ABILITIES ARE POSSIBLE, THEY'RE OUTSIDE OF
MY SKILL SET. I HAVE HEARD THE A-ING-TII MONKS
MAY HAVE THE ABILITY TO FOLD SPACE.
                                        —LUKE

The anima governs life, and it is through this state that Force healing is possible.

But to sever the Force—that is something rare. To sever the Force is to trigger a mass die-off of a victim's midi-chlorians—not enough to kill but enough to take a Jedi's power. It could be that the Jedi of old knew this feat, but if so they did not understand its underpinnings. Severing the Force is the inverse of what I have done when inducing midi-chlorians to create life. It is far easier to achieve.

The pneuma governs consciousness. Through this I am convinced that the energy pattern we know as self-awareness can be preserved, and imprinted a second time into the neural pathways of a different brain. This process would be simplest with a cloned body that is identical to the subject's own, though in theory any advanced biological form would prove sufficient. Body swapping of this nature is riskier than simply sustaining one's own life through midi-chlorian manipulation. In dire emergency, however, it could serve as an escape against oblivion.

The original body and the clone host. Identical brain structure facilitates thought transfer.

I am pleased my Master began this work, for it is far more than an escape! The dark side ravages the flesh I believe that I might sustain my life only by transferring it into the body of a cloned host.

# Transcending Death

The act of transferring consciousness between bodies touches on a subject that still troubles me. The patterns that define each mind can be stored in the pneuma field, but these patterns degrade almost instantly if they are not anchored in a new biological form. The speed of this degradation is so rapid that it seems to render the argument for life after death moot. But yet, I have always been one to follow the evidence. . . .

All beings are afraid of oblivion. Every culture has written fables to assure themselves that death is not the end. Even the Jedi do this. Through midi-chlorians, they believe they have a connection to the universe's fundamental energies that others do not. Therefore, I am reluctant to dismiss their histories too rapidly.

During the Great Sith War, Jedi combatants were said to have vanished at the moment of their deaths, with the cells of their bodies sublimating into energy. It must be noted that although I have witnessed the death of Jedi, I have never witnessed this phenomenon.

Some of these Jedi were said to have returned as pure consciousness, communicating specific and verifiable information to the living. Ghost stories are so common they are laughable, but the pneuma leads me to believe that such a thing is possible.

*I have studied the art of the dark transfer, a technique later perfected by the Jedi Ashka Boda, whom I tortured and killed. I have ordered the production of inert clones of my body. One day I will have an inexhaustible supply of fresh forms, and the means to pass between them when the flesh proves weak.*

I'VE SEEN YODA, BEN, AND MY FATHER RETURN FROM DEATH.

THE FORCE IS A WELCOMING PLACE, FAR LARGER THAN PLAGUEIS'S ATTEMPTS TO MEASURE AND MINIMIZE IT.

—LUKE

## The Netherworld and Chaos

How mental patterns persist beyond our physical minds remains an enigma. Thought degrades into randomness in less than a minute. To hold awareness longer than that—and to appear to others in the physical world while retaining both visual and auditory aspects—is a remarkable feat, if true. I have read that the Lorekeepers of the Whills have perfected this, but the Whills remain a frustrating puzzle for those who wish to learn more about them.

One thing is clear: although such a phenomenon technically meets the definition of life after death, it is not supernatural. The unimaginative always ascribe their own motivations to independent phenomena, including those who believe the Force has a consciousness and a will. In fact, though midi-chlorians share a collective mind, the Force itself could not possibly know or care about the welfare of intelligent life. My goal, therefore, is to separate genuine insight from hyperbole. I do not know how the Jedi of the past achieved the supposed miracle of retaining their awareness after death, but I know it was not through supplication and prayer.

However, the fact that individual identities are absorbed into the pneuma at the moment of their deaths explains several associated legends. The Jedi, for example, speak of the netherworld beyond death, a realm that is vague on detail but said to be a place of utmost peace. Similarly, Chaos is where dead Sith Lords are believed to dwell in torment. At least according to legend, those who are too weak to punish their enemies during their lifetime will be forced to hold on to their grudges and to live on in Chaos, plotting but never being able to exact their revenge.

the peace of the netherworld? It is easily understood as the reaction of a mind that finds itself dissipating into the hum of background energy and accepts its fate without pain or fear. Minds that are less inclined to accept their loss of identity will fight to keep their grasp on order. These stronger minds will recoil as their constituent threads are pulled apart, and they will perceive their imminent dissolution as Chaos.

I wonder if my Master knew the ancient Naboo legend that speaks of a realm called Chaos, blocked by a sextet of impenetrable barriers. If Chaos exists, then it takes a sufficiently determined mind to overcome it and return to life. Let the weak have their peace.

## Sith Spirits

The most accessible lore concerning life after death is found in the Holocrons of the Sith. Indeed, the Sith Holocrons are said to contain the spirits of their builders, and these spirits interact with users as holographic gatekeepers. But all of this is sleight of hand, a programmable artificial intelligence that wears the face of a long-dead lord.

More interesting are the tales of Sith ghosts said to haunt everything from the tombs of Korriban to the relics inside Coruscant's Great Galactic Museum. Is it possible that these Masters of the dark side succeeded in preserving their awareness? If so, can they still be queried for their secrets? Unfortunately, I have been to Korriban, and I am not convinced that these tales hold truth.

ANYONE WHO DISMISSES THE EXISTENCE OF THE SITH SPIRITS HAS NEVER FOUGHT ONE. IT TOOK EVERY JEDI IN MY ACADEMY TO DEFEAT THE SPIRIT OF EXAR KUN.
        —LUKE

The spirits of Korriban are quite real. Indeed, on one occasion they nearly killed me. But I agree with my Master in this observation —the dead Dark Lords are evasive in their speech and are ultimately treacherous.

140

The Tomb of Hakagram Graush remained silent to my queries, and the throne where Sorzus Syn once sat contained no mocking, imperious specter. I was ready to conclude that the tales are merely diversions for the credulous, but as I boarded my ship in the Valley of the Dark Lords, I beheld a vision of the Sith Lord Marka Ragnos. The apparition challenged my claim to the Sith title and railed against my plan to dismantle the traditions of Korriban. But the vision of Ragnos would not answer my questions nor my delineated inquiries. He snarled and disappeared in a whirl of smoke. It is possible that the entire episode simply played out in my mind.

The illusion of Marka Ragnos could not offer proof of its own existence.

There is one spirit encounter that would truly intrigue me, however. I would enjoy questioning my Master, Darth Tenebrous, to see if he anticipated my growing power, and whether he knew I might destory him on Bal'demnic. I wonder what Tenebrous would think of all his apprentice has achieved since that day.

# The Prophecy of the Chosen One

The beliefs of the Jedi are expressed in ritual and storytelling. Plain language somehow eludes those who have grown up tightly wrapped in tradition.

The Jedi await the coming of a savior, a prophesied Chosen One who will destroy the Sith and bring balance to the Force. The Jedi tell tales of Mortis, a place of impossible geography inside the angles of a gargantuan monolith. The three all-powerful beings of Mortis can assume strange shapes and exemplify the dark side, the light side, and the principle of balance.

The legend of Mortis has inspired much folklore.

Compelling? It is debatable, but at the very least it is an adequate way to illustrate an allegorical point. Day coexists with night, for example, and construction is always followed by ruin. Yet many of the Jedi treat the legend of Mortis as literal truth. They believe that the Chosen One will prevent these gods and demons from tearing the universe asunder—that their champion will be a vessel of pure Force energy.

So we come back to midi-chlorians. These organisms allow beings to live and provide a connection to the Force. If bred in sufficient quantities, midi-chlorians can even conceive a new life form and bestow upon it powers greater than any Jedi has ever dreamed, generating a vergence in the Force.

If I induce midi-chlorians to create such a being, my handiwork would fit all the descriptions of their Chosen One. But he would be an agent of my will. How fitting that the misguided reliance on superstition could lead to a Sith creation that is hailed by the Jedi as a savior.

This prophecy will never come to pass. Under my reign, the Sith will hold their authority forever.

PLAGUEIS MADE THE MISTAKE OF BELIEVING THAT IF SOMETHING ISN'T LITERALLY TRUE, THEN IT HAS NO VALUE. I DON'T KNOW THE JEDI LEGENDS WELL, BUT THE BALANCE OF THE FORCE IS A SUBJECT TO BE STUDIED, NOT DISMISSED.

—LUKE

# The Culmination of the Sith'ari

The Sith have their religion, too. Since the time of Korriban's savage primitives, our Order has become encumbered by rituals in the way that a starship accumulates mynocks. This ends with me. I will replace those beliefs with truth, rationality, and the rule of the gifted.

Yet the prophecy of the Sith'ari still holds some interest. Prophecies are generally wishful thinking, but because midi-chlorians have the ability to tap the aperion, any tugs on space-time can be interpreted as futuresight. The fact that the Sith created their own savior myth is predictable, but the prophecy states that a being will arise who is free from restrictions and who will destroy the Sith only to make them stronger than before. These statements seem uniquely specific to the actions I am taking now.

I am free from blind obedience to symbols and mysticism. I will end the traditions that have bound the Sith throughout their history. I have unlocked the secrets of life, and by doing so I will enable long-term plans to ensure Sith dominance for centuries. I am not a creature of superstition. But if the robes of the Sith'ari fit, I see no reason not to claim them.

Plagueis failed to achieve his goals because he did not remain strong. Such blindness for one who claimed deep insight.

*Looking back on these words from a remove of nearly twenty years, I should have moved more quickly in silencing the Senate. That contemptible body became a cesspool of grandstanding simpletons.*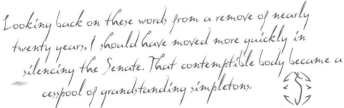

# ABSOLUTE POWER

## By Darth Sidious

The writings I have collected in this volume appear in their original forms. Many are fragments of what once were longer works, but the preservation of what remains is less important than the recognition of how they led to my new vision of the Sith Order. The following three books—The Weakness of Inferiors, The Book of Anger, and The Manipulation of Life—present how I achieved absolute power, how I shall maintain it through the agency of my Galactic Empire, and how I will reshape the galaxy throughout the ages to come.

*So simple in concept, yet I am bound by the incompetence of others. I trust that my commanders will stifle dissent, but frequently it grows louder. Had I not foreseen my eternal triumph, I might be troubled.*

# THE WEAKNESS OF INFERIORS

The Empire has only begun to be built. But its foundation is the anger of the dark side. Although the mindless subjects know nothing of this shadowy majesty, the true power of the Empire originates with its Emperor. The promises laid out by the Rule of Two have been fulfilled. The Sith have been brought to glory, and the Jedi to destruction.

As Darth Bane and Mother Talzin knew, the weakness of inferiors is self-evident. The weak do not understand the Force. They are ignorant and lack power, but they may still be exploited for gain. No ruler can manage an entity as complex as the populated galaxy without knowing how to manipulate others.

Fear is the spark that drove my march to power. Even now it fuels the engine of my Empire. The weak must be trained to fear the consequences of betrayal. They must dread that their neighbor's loyalty is greater than their own. The anxious will whip themselves into hysterical nationalism without further prompting. For fear is self-perpetuating. The weak live in terror that they will be judged for their failings and be put on display—that they will be punished. It is a belief that should not be discouraged.

PALPATINE WAS WRONG. THOSE WHO LIVE UNDER FEAR CAN'T WAIT TO THROW OFF THAT YOKE. I'VE SEEN THE FOOTAGE TAKEN AFTER THE NEWS OF THE EMPEROR'S DEATH AT ENDOR HIT THE NEWSNETS. THE PEOPLE OF CORUSCANT CELEBRATED LOUDER AND LONGER THAN ANYONE.
—LUKE

It is maddening, educating this rabble. With the Empire now nearly a generation old, my Imperial governors should at least understand the principle of the law of fear, yet I would have better success trying to teach Aurebesh to a Gungan.

Coruscant under my rule. Darth Bane beheld it in a vision, but I will see the reality.

## THE FALSE WAR

Fear was a necessary component in destroying the Jedi and burning away the putrefying vestiges of the Republic. But first I had to create that fear—fear of revolution, of destruction, and of death. I had to create a war on a massive scale.

My apprentice Count Dooku rallied star systems to his banner, inflaming passions among Rim citizens. This naturally deepened the fears of Core residents, who clamored for protection like brush-kits mewling for their mothers. The clone army I had prepared was met with applause and relief. And so began the Clone Wars.

It did not matter at all that I dictated orders to the Separatists through my

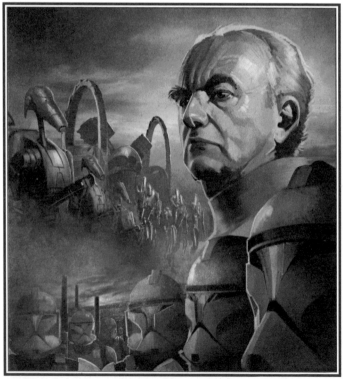

SEPARATISTS AND REPUBLIC SOLDIERS STOOD UNKNOWINGLY ATOP A DEJARIK BOARD.
I CONTROLLED THE CONFLICT AND ITS ENDGAME.

apprentice. Nor that every Republic victory was followed with a carefully planned defeat. The benefits of the false war were countless. From the clone army came a battle fleet and an arsenal of new mechanized weapons of war. Overnight, the Republic had a class of military elites who swore their loyalty to the Supreme Chancellor. The Senators feared that being painted as disloyal would make them unelectable, so they supported measures to dismantle all checks on centralized power. On the opposite side, the Trade Federation, the Commerce Guild, and other corporate conglomerates joined together to protect their profits. They unknowingly pledged their allegiance to the Sith.

The Jedi did not want war, but they had little choice. They had to join the fight lest they face public scorn. There on the front lines, my war struck down my enemies and shredded their morals until they were on the brink of the dark side. The Jedi were never the true heroes. I saw to that by manipulating the HoloNet. The people were led to fear the Jedi's arrogance and strange power. By crafting the news, the clone troopers and their noble chancellor became the fearless heroes of the Republic.

When the time came for the Jedi to be eliminated, the public did not mourn them. When the Senate learned that the Jedi had attempted a coup and needed to be exterminated, they responded with absolute certainty. And when the people saw smoke rising from the Jedi Temple, they felt relief.

Even though I'm reading Palpatine's own words, I still can't believe this truth. According to every historical record I've ever seen, the factions fighting the Clone Wars had no idea of this master plan.
—LUKE

## THE USEFUL BUREAUCRATS

My Master, Darth Plagueis, developed an obsession with midi-chlorians, neglecting his greatest talent—manipulating the strings that kept the galaxy from degenerating into anarchy. As a key figure in the InterGalactic Banking Clan, he was well acquainted with the business leaders and politicians who shaped the very galaxy—yet for all their power, not one of them was recognizable to general citizens.

Control of this invisible steering committee is vital to the rule of the Empire, for their fortunes are tied to the regime's success. The corporate entities, the Senate, the HoloNet, and the military are all under my control. The loss of any one would undermine my central authority.

There are, of course, unspoken members of this vital committee. Nothing could be accomplished without the tacit support of petty crime lords. Chief among these are the Hutt cartels, the Bothan Spy Networks, the Black Sun underworld syndicate, and the Bounty Hunters Guild. These groups are not in any measurable way different from the bankers and traders. They will remain content as long as profits are strong. But fear must be stoked from time to time. They must be reminded that doing business with Rebels and seditionists leads to punishment and financial ruin.

The military families of the Core hold influence over their sectors and have long hungered for a strong hand at the top. Although the Clone Wars have ended, I have heard no whisperings from anyone wishing to dismantle our armies. I will fortify the Galactic Empire, and my authority, with the greatest strength the galaxy has ever seen.

TIE fighters will scream through the skies while stormtroopers and armored walkers will round up dissenters on any planet

*Love of money is apparently stronger than the fear of death. A few of these traitors have cut deals to arm the Rebels. When I eliminate an executive, the replacement is much less likely to make the same mistake.*

*In the years since I first recorded these thoughts, I have come to despise the Bounty Hunters Guild. Boba Fett and those like him can be unpredictable to the point of exasperation. But Count Dooku and Lord Vader have both made intelligent use of these bandits.*

unwilling to submit to my rule. Imperial Star Destroyers will orbit above population centers, waiting for orders to open fire if their leaders fail to see the benefits of becoming an Imperial possession.

Finally, my Death Star will be the ultimate battle station and the personification of fear. Its weapon will shatter planets and extinguish all will to fight across the galaxy. When complete, the Death Star will spell an end to the insignificant threats of rebellions and organized protests. *The designer has been tortured and the architects executed. Tarkin is fortunate to have died along with the other commanders when the Death Star exploded. He had far too much ambition, and his days were numbered.*

*I may have been the one who fired the shot, but the Force itself wanted to purge the galaxy of the Death Star. It was the embodiment of everything that's wrong with the dark side.*

*—LUKE*

WITH THE HOLONET, THE SYNDICATES, AND THE CORPORATIONS IN MY FIST I CAN DICTATE ANY TRUTH OF MY CHOOSING. THOSE WHO STILL RESIST WILL SURRENDER WHEN CONFRONTED WITH MILITARY POWER

## Hiding in Plain Sight

The galaxy is free of Jedi, and the citizens rejoice. Therefore it would be foolish to replace their regime with an identical system led by the Sith, at least publicly.

The weak do not understand the Force. They venerate those who appear to be ordinary people like themselves. They cheered at the news that a resolute old man had survived a Jedi assassination attempt. In Palpatine, an ordinary Senator from Naboo, they see a model of human achievement.

My apprentice and other agents of my will are fearsome embodiments of the dark side. Mere rumors of their presence are enough to frighten citizens into obedience. But those same citizens must not know that a Sith Lord has constructed the Galactic Empire until it is too late.

The weak-minded see what they wish. They are complicit in their own deception.

But that hidden truth in no way diminishes my triumph. The Sith have long operated from the shadows, and the thousand-year wait of Darth Bane is over. The Sith have exacted their revenge. The galaxy praises the Empire, and the feeble-minded are not worthy of understanding its true origins.

Like Darth Bane and my Master before me, I have honed the tools of deception. Darth Bane kept a low profile, but it was Darth Plagueis who, as the public face of the InterGalactic Banking Clan, shaped the economies of entire regions.

In truth, everyone wears a mask. When speaking to others, a false persona can charm, seduce, or frighten. A Sith knows that all interactions are masked. It is no great difficulty to don multiple masks when the situation demands it.

All beings want to make sense of their reality, but none of them wish to think too deeply. They gravitate toward words that confirm their existing suspicions.

In my decades as Ambassador, Senator, and Supreme Chancellor, I did not once encounter an exception to this rule. It was true whether I was reminding the Senate of the need for war powers or <u>sitting across from Master Yoda</u> and convincing him to send more Jedi Knights into harm's way. None suspected the duplicity of my identity. In fact, so convinced were the Jedi of their superior insight that they were the easiest to deceive.

THAT THE SITH PULLED OFF SUCH A MONUMENTAL DECEPTION BACK WHEN THE JEDI WERE AT THEIR MOST POWERFUL . . . LET'S JUST SAY I'M KEEPING MY EYES OPEN FOR TROUBLE.

—LUKE

PALPATINE'S PROPAGANDISTS WORKED SO WELL THAT MANY PEOPLE BORN DURING THE DARK TIMES BELIEVED THE JEDI WERE A MYTH.

—LUKE

# THE BOOK OF ANGER

Through the principles of anger, I will structure and maintain my Empire. The writings of Darth Malgus confirm that anger, combined with will, is the key to power. When anger intensifies to rage, it is unstoppable. Malgus submitted utterly to the dark side, and doing so made him an exemplary warrior. His battlefield feats have never been duplicated.

It must be understood that anger can be funneled through the body and released near the heart at the "vital gate." The destruction that can be unleashed by this method is immense. Thousands of enemies can be annihilated in a single act of malice.

In time, the channeled anger of the dark side will prove just as destructive as the Death Star. There will no longer be a need for costly constructions. Already, I have perfected the Force maelstrom, which creates an invulnerable energy sphere to block incoming attacks while bombarding enemies with debris and electrifying them with bolts of lightning.

This technique can be increased into a Force Storm. The churning energy mass of a Force Storm can consume

MALGUS HARNESSED THE FORCE MAELSTROM TO ANNIHILATE THE UNREADY.

One of the Emperor's Force Storms destroyed the Alliance base on the moon of Da Soocha and the entire fleet above it. Every day I'm reminded how lucky we are that Palpatine is lost to chaos forever. —LUKE

everything it touches, for at its eye is pure hate. Just as a black hole devours a star, this storm can swallow armies and fold space. It may take decades to master this art, but once I have perfected it, I will be invincible.

Anger has more uses than personal strength. A strong ruler knows that fear can keep commoners in line, but anger can weaken enemies.

Indeed, my subjects fear me, but that fear will lead to anger. And anger will make my Empire strong. However, anger directed toward authority is dangerous. It must be channeled toward other, weaker subjects. By encouraging fear of the exotic and the unusual, a regime can be strengthened. The Empire has uniformity in its symbols and its ideology, which makes it easier to shame those who do not belong and to make them the objects of a galaxy's rage.

The Republic's alien species are the simplest targets. Most humans of the Core already despise looking into their multiple eyes or listening to their clicking, buzzing languages. They hate their bewildering customs and their sharp stench. Coruscant is a seething boil of species, but humans far outnumber any other species. It is an ideal place to sow seeds of suspicion—to instill the idea that those who don't conform are the enemy and enemies must be destroyed. By making the powerless a target, the people will not threaten the one in power. On the contrary, the ruler will be venerated as a hero for exposing the weak.

As Darth Bane instituted the Rule of Two, so I will begin the Rule of One. The Sith will now be sustained by one— one to hold the power and others, talented in the Force, to execute my will as dark side agents.

Although the Jedi Order has been obliterated, many Force-sensitives have survived. Those who still hold to the belief that there is virtue in "peace"—or in closing one's self off to sensation—will be made to conform. They must find value in the ways of the dark.

Unleashing their anger is fundamental for drawing them into my fold as well as for them to gain an understanding of the dark side. For it is in anger that Force-users are strongest. Once tapped, this emotion can turn idealists into slaves. Even those with brightly burning passions—those who vow to resist with their dying breath—can be broken in three simple steps.

First, they must be tempted. The strong willed always have something they desire, or something they possess that they fear to lose. They will see their drive to protect this item as noble. By encouraging this delusion, a puppet is created.

Second, the puppets must be tested. By creating an immediate danger or placing the subjects in peril, they will be forced to make a decision. Crazed by fear and the mere thought of losing what they hold dear, they will do anything that is asked of them, if only to preserve their most cherished desires.

Third, they must be forced to submit. A moment will arise when they will take a step too far. In panic or fear, they will hurt others or commit a crime in such a way the outside world will never forgive. After that moment, there is no return from the dark side. Some who have been ensnared will choose to end their lives. Most, however, will accept their role as new warriors of the dark side. One life has ended, and a better one has begun.

As the new Rule of One is enacted, I will be free to enlist a throng of dark side followers. These talented mimics will be trained to replicate a

MY FATHER BROKE THIS CYCLE WITH HIS FINAL ACTION—
A-TONEMENT. BY DESTROYING PALPATINE HE RESTORED
BALANCE TO THE FORCE. —LUKE

Grand Inquisitor Torbin is the latest of these fools to perish. A bomb? A speeder crash? DROWNING? In death my Inquisitors are making a mockery of their Empire's infallibility.

smattering of my abilities yet will never take even a fraction of my authority.

The Inquisitorius is an arm of Imperial Intelligence tasked with extracting information through torture. The most effective will serve as Grand Inquisitors, and the best of those will be selected as Emperor's Hands. These elite agents will be handpicked for loyalty and stealth. They shall be unseen enforcers across the breadth of my vast dominion.

The red-robed Royal Guard will protect me from those who think themselves worthy of an audience with their Emperor. Within their ranks, a few who are in touch with the Force will comprise a rarefied warrior unit called the Shadow Guard.

The captured Padawans and survivors from the Jedi Service Corps are less gifted in the Force, but they will serve me nonetheless as Dark Side Adepts. Until I have use for them, they shall remain on Byss, where their connection to the Force will intensify the planet's growing nexus of dark side potency.

MY HEART ACHES FOR THE FORCE-USERS WHO LIVED DURING PALPATINE'S DARK TIMES. BEING OPEN ABOUT THEIR GIFTS MEANT SERVING A MONSTER. LUCKILY SOME OF THEM, LIKE MARA, FOUND A NEW PATH.
—LUKE

MY EMPEROR'S HANDS ARE MY PRIMARY AGENTS, FOLLOWED BY THE SHADOW GUARDS AND THEN THE RANKS OF THE INQUISITORIUS.

# THE MANIPULATION OF LIFE

The future of my Empire is found in the mysteries of life—how to hold on to it so that my reign will never end. And how to twist it to create colossi that will do my bidding. Not even nature can stand in my way.

I have mastered the dark side arts of deception, fear, and anger, but the Science of Darkness represented by the writings of Sorzus Syn and Darth Plagueis is open for exploration. Amusingly, the philosophies of the two authors could not be more opposed.

Both Sith Lords understood that living things are not special. They are a resource to be harvested and shaped by the powerful. Through the dark side, I can make many new shapes.

The alchemy developed by Syn is being perfected on Byss, where my Dark Side Adepts join their potent skills to warp life on a broad scale. My monstrous chrysalides, with their magnificent metal-piercing fangs, guard the ramparts of my citadel. My mute Imperial sentinels stand by my throne, their annihilated minds and enslaved wills clear evidence the dark side can manipulate clones for any imaginative purpose. Although alchemy can create perfect beings, I have designed weaknesses into all of these creations. The flaws are minute and known only to me. It would not do for any creature to be stronger than its creator.

These experiments will lead to greater things—opportunities for me to create new beings of my own design. What then will separate me from the gods of Naboo myth?

The philosophy of creating monsters is applicable to the most fundamental elements of life. Darth Plagueis focused much too narrowly on midi-chlorians, but he was right about a great many things. The dark side consumes the physical body—just as mine became

THE GALACTIC EMPIRE IS MY CREATION. ENTIRE GENERATIONS WILL LIVE AND DIE UNDER MY RULE.

misshapen after the attempted Jedi assassination—but the mind can be preserved. Through the art of dark transfer, I will soon move myself to a younger body cloned from my own cells.

I will achieve immortality. Even if I am killed, I will return from the chaos of non-being to restored physical life. This, even my Master could not achieve. I knew it was so when I halted his breathing and watched the light vanish from his eyes. He sought the secret of life, to live forever, but I took his life. I remain the ultimate Sith.

Throughout the eras, the Sith foretold of a being who would destroy their Order and rebuild it stronger than before. I do not care about ancient prophecies. The approval of the dead is meaningless. Yet it is clear that the *Sith'ari* could be no other than me.

The Imperial age has begun. I have centuries to expound on my philosophies, yet all knowledge flows from the dark side writings collected here. Let these pages mark the inception of the first *Book of Sith*.

ISBN: 9781781166178

*Book of Sith: Secrets from the Dark Side* is published by Titan Books
A division of Titan Publishing Group Ltd., 144 Southwark St.,
London, SE1 0UP
www.titanbooks.com

Published by arrangement with becker&meyer!
www.beckermeyer.com

Edited by Delia Greve
Designed by Rosanna Brockley
Production coordination by Jen Marx
Managing editor Michael del Rosario

Lucasfilm Ltd.
Executive Editor: J.W. Rinzler
Art Director: Troy Alders
Keeper of the Holocron: Leland Chee
Director of Publishing: Carol Roeder

Manufactured in China

Text and annotations written by Daniel Wallace
Illustrations by: Paul Allan Ballard: pp. 131–142; Jeff Carlisle: pp. 50–64; Chris Reiff: pp. 79, 81, 85, 88, and 89; Chris Trevas: pp. 67–77; Russell Walks: pp. 99–127; Terryl Whitlatch: pp. 36–39; and Aristia/Hive Studios: pp. 11–34, 40–43, 80, 82, 84, 86, 91–96, 145–159

10 9 8 7 6 5 4 3 2 1

Did you enjoy this book? We love to hear from our readers.
Please e-mail us at: readerfeedback@titanemail.com
or write to Reader Feedback at the above address.

12396